# The QUALITY of LEICESTER

# The QUALITY of LEICESTER

Researched and written
by
Michael Taylor

Design and photography
by
George Wilson

Published by

*The problem of how to keep traditional towns alive, without destroying what makes life worth living in them, remains. There is no easy answer, no grand, sweeping solution. But to love one's own town and to learn everything one can about its history and what gives it its individuality, is at least a step in the right direction.*

Mark Girouard *The English Town 1990*

Designed and produced by Leicester City Council
Environment and Development Department

First published in 1993 by Leicester City Council
Revised Second Edition published 1997



Text set in Bembo 11 on 14pt

Electronic Page Make-up and Output by
Greenshires Creative Colour Ltd.

Printed by Greenshires Creative Colour Ltd, Leicester.



ISBN 1 901156 10 9 The Quality of Leicester

# *Acknowledgements*

THE QUALITY OF LEICESTER has been produced by the Urban Design Group in the Environment and Development Department of Leicester City Council. It was researched and written by Michael Taylor, Building Conservation Officer in the Group. George Wilson, Presentation Assistant, designed the book and took many of the photographs. The location maps and other work were by Jeremy Crooks, and Arthur Barnacle helped with production of the page layouts. Other members of the Department helped with research, organisation, editing, proofreading and word processing.

Additional photographs were taken by Ian Davis of the Council's Photographic Unit and Richard Payne of the Urban Design Group. Some of the photographic material was supplied from stock by the Photographic Unit and by Leicestershire Museums, Arts and Records Service. Repro-proofs of the photographs were printed by Vasant Kalyani of the Photographic Unit.

Information on housing renewal was researched by Lynn Senior, Urban Management Officer (South Highfields) in the Council's Housing Department, and by Alison Bowen in the Environment and Development Department. Phil Spiers, Senior Structural Engineer in the Commercial Services Department, researched the material on bridges.

The Race Relations Section of the Chief Executive's Department read and commented on the draft text. Mark Bentley, the Council's Public Relations Manager, advised on the presentation of the book and suggested the title. The Council's Reprographics Manager, Kevin Vernon, smoothed the path from the production and design stage to printing.

A number of local experts gave their time and attention in reading and correcting the draft text. Yolanda Courtney of Newarke Houses Museum and her husband Paul, Bob Rutland of Jewry Wall Museum, members of the former Leicestershire Archaeological Unit, and Peter Swallow and John Stanley of De Montfort University, all helped to polish the text and pointed out potential errors.

Pat Kirkham of De Montfort University supplied the material about Harry Peach. Patrick Davis, Keith Dickens, Michael Eaton, Richard Gill, Alan Kind, Joan Skinner, Douglas Smith, and many others answered our requests for information or checked or verified points for us.

Geoff Pyrah kindly gave his time to compiling the index for the 1997 edition.

The staff of Leicestershire County Records Office were most helpful in making drawings and other information available.

Leicestershire County Council (particularly the Property and Museums, Arts and Records Departments), the Parochial Church Councils of St Denys, St James the Greater, St John the Baptist, St Mary de Castro and St Nicholas, and many other owners of property, gave us access to their buildings to take photographs, often at considerable inconvenience to themselves. The management and staff of Norman and Underwood Ltd., provided facilities for us to photograph their work. Freda Hussain, Principal of Moat Community College, allowed us to take photographs at the College.

# *Preface to First Edition*

THIS IS NOT a book about 'heritage'. It is a picture of the elements which make up a changing city, one which respects and looks after the evidence of its history as a foundation for building its future.

The book has several aims. Most of all *The Quality of Leicester* is for the citizens of Leicester. The City may be so familiar to us that we stop looking at it, and stop seeing its special qualities. We hope that the text and pictures will open everyone's eyes to Leicester's rich, varied, and very individual character. Protecting and developing that character is not just a matter for the City Council but for everyone who lives or works in Leicester.

For architects and developers the book is a statement of what the City Council feels makes Leicester a distinctive place with qualities to be acknowledged, reflected and enhanced by new development. The book will show that using the established character of the City as a starting point can produce original buildings which help to reinforce Leicester's individuality.

We hope that *The Quality of Leicester* will also appeal to visitors and will serve as a welcome to our City and an invitation to look at and enjoy Leicester's buildings, streets and open spaces.

Councillor P.A. Soulsby
*Leader, Leicester City Council*

Councillor B.K. Shore
*Chair, Planning Committee,*
*Leicester City Council*

# *Preface to Second Edition*

SINCE THE QUALITY OF LEICESTER was first published in 1993 nearly 5,000 copies have been sold. Many of these have been taken and sent abroad and the book has acted as an ambassador for Leicester all over the world. It has been the subject of reviews, radio and television coverage, exhibitions, and many talks and presentations. The book has had successful 'spin-offs' in the form of postcards, a poster, and limited edition prints of some of the photographs.

In 1993 *The Quality of Leicester* received a commendation in the Royal Town Planning Institute Awards for Planning Achievement.

Recognition in this way is very rewarding but the focus of the book remains firmly fixed here in Leicester. The aims set out in the Preface to the first edition of *The Quality of Leicester* remain as important as ever. The planning of the City takes place within a framework of local democracy and the best guarantee of an environment of high quality is a public who are aware of the importance of quality and who demand high standards in conservation and new development.

So the most gratifying comments we have received have been those of Leicester people who have perhaps noticed some aspect or detail of the environment for the first time through the book. If a book can help Leicester people to see and enjoy the City's environment, then *The Quality of Leicester* can help to protect and build on the quality of Leicester.

Councillor P.A. Soulsby
*Leader, Leicester City Council*

Councillor Ted Cassidy
*Chair, Environment and Development Committee, Leicester City Council*

Councillor Roy Stuttard
*Chair, Urban Management Sub-Committee Leicester City Council*

Church of St. John the Baptist,
Clarendon Park Road, the chancel

# *Contents*

# 1
# *Introduction*

BRITAIN is a small country but has great variety. Travelling for an hour or two can bring differences in the landscape and in the buildings that form part of it. These differences reflect changes in rock and soil and in the way past generations have shaped the countryside, villages, towns and cities. Each area and settlement has its own particular story which is reflected in a unique mixture of landscape and buildings. This diversity is priceless and, to maintain it, the special character of every part of Britain must be appreciated and cherished. The story told by an industrial city such as Leicester is as important as that of a cathedral city or spa town. *The Quality of Leicester* will show how Leicester's story is reflected today in its streets and buildings.

A city is a patchwork pieced together over centuries. Parts of it will bear the imprint of later additions and changes. They will each have a layout, building styles and materials characteristic of their locality and reflecting the lives and work of local people. These elements add up to the *character* of a city: the qualities which make it different from every other place.

This individual quality is formed by people living, working and enjoying themselves and, in the process, continuing to shape the city. The names of the Norman lords who built Leicester Castle have been passed down to the present in history books. The masons and carpenters who built the Castle hall in the twelfth century are forgotten but their work, even though changed by later generations, is as durable as the written accounts of their employers' lives. A city is a record of countless human activities and decisions.

It was only in the twentieth century that those activities and decisions were guided by a system of

ABOVE Leicester Caribbean Carnival 1992

RIGHT Slate headstones, St Mary de Castro Churchyard

FACING PAGE New Walk looking south

planning laws and regulations. This is not to say that the development of the City was previously haphazard or unplanned. Planning, in its broadest sense, has been shaping the City since long before Planning Acts were introduced. But planning by the local authorities, particularly under the laws introduced in 1948, has helped Leicester to cope with the enormous changes this century has brought.

People from Asia, Africa and the Caribbean, and their Leicester-born children, give a variety and vitality to Leicester's character which could not have been dreamed of even in the 1940s. There is nothing new in people coming from abroad to live here. Romans, Saxons, Normans and Danes all settled in Leicester after moving from other countries. There has been a Jewish community here for many centuries. During the 1930s and 1940s people from continental Europe established their homes and community life in Leicester. Architectural styles from France, Germany, the Netherlands and even America have influenced the City we know today.

Familiar buildings and streets from recent decades may seem less valuable than the legacy of earlier centuries but many of them will come to be seen as important in the future. This underlines the importance of quality in new development and of recognising the value of the work of the recent past.

Architecture and the environment are often discussed in the press and on radio and television. Deeply held views are expressed, particularly about the merits of modern architecture. This debate is valuable in focusing public attention on the environment but often seems to be largely concerned with architectural style. There were similar passionate debates about style in the nineteenth century and it is now hard for us to understand the depth of feelings expressed then. Looking back at the Victorian era, we can see that great buildings were produced in a variety of styles and this diversity gave richness to the architecture of that period. This is a theme which will be illustrated in the chapters to follow.

Despite all the changes that have affected it over centuries Leicester still shows signs of what it must have been like before it became an industrial town. Much of the city centre keeps its mediaeval street layout. In the suburbs the centres of what were once distinct villages remain. At the beginning of the nineteenth century many Leicester people worked at hosiery machines in their own homes. The change to factory-based industry left much of the small scale of

Braunstone Village: Cressida Place 1859

Leicester intact. Nineteenth century Leicester was a cautious town. Small areas of land were developed at a time and there was little call for grandiose monuments or expensive civic splendour. As a result Leicester grew to prosperity while keeping much of the character of a Georgian market town. In the past this might have been seen as a lack of character. But this is part of the record which has been passed down to us of the City's story: what makes Leicester a special place.

*The Quality of Leicester* will describe particular places in the City and analyse the clues they give to Leicester's history and the contribution they make to the City's character. The order will be roughly chronological but the development of the City was not a tidy process and a chapter focusing mainly on one era may contain buildings from others. The growth of Leicester was particularly vigorous in the second half of the nineteenth century and the chapters dealing with that period will show some of the many parallel themes in the Victorian development of the City.

This book is not a history of Leicester, nor a catalogue of its buildings. Rather we will try to show what the special quality of Leicester is: highly individual and fragile but the starting point for the development of a city moving into its third millennium.

# PART ONE

Jewry Wall

*The next six chapters will look at parts of Leicester which reflect the City's history from its origins through to the end of the Middle Ages. There is evidence of dramatic events and Leicester's character still shows the influence of the institutions which controlled the town and the surrounding countryside through periods of stability or gradual evolution.*

# 2
# *Origins of a City*

ALTHOUGH PEOPLE had already lived in the area for thousands of years, Leicester grew from a late Iron Age settlement on the eastern bank of the River Soar near to where West Bridge now stands. Here, over two thousand years ago, people of Celtic origin set up a village. They were members of the Corieltauvi tribe whose territory covered part of the East Midlands and Warwickshire. Corieltauvian coins displayed in Jewry Wall Museum suggest that they had an organised way of life and a keen sense of artistry and workmanship.

For the Romans, the river crossing and the existing settlement made Leicester an important strategic point. The garrison they established eventually developed into a middle-ranking town, Ratae Corieltauvorum, the capital of the Corieltauvi tribe and something like a county town today. It would have had a set of public buildings and spaces to reflect its importance and to bring something of the Roman way of life to the northern colony. These public buildings were built in stone and brick to show their purpose and status. The baths were the centre of Roman social life and it is part of the bath-house which has survived as a link between the Roman town and the modern city. In the 1930s the baths site was excavated by archaeologists and the layout of the walls marked out in the low stonework seen at the Jewry Wall site today. There would have been many smaller buildings in the Roman town. But it is those built in the tile-like Roman brick, sandstone from Danehills and Derbyshire, limestone from Evington, or igneous rock from Charnwood, of which the most evidence has survived.

The neat brickwork and stonework of Jewry Wall, particularly the brick over the arched opening, show

ABOVE LEFT The Blackfriars Pavement

ABOVE RIGHT Roman column bases in St Nicholas' Churchyard

RIGHT Roman tile/brick with footprints of child and a dog, Jewry Wall Museum

FACING PAGE
TOP Corieltauvian gold coin found in Leicester:design shows a horse: actual size 19mm diameter (photo: Leicester Museums Service)

BOTTOM The Blackfriars Pavement, Roman, Jewry Wall Museum

the quality of the building skills which the Roman invaders brought with them. Wall plaster, painted with intricate patterns, is evidence that decorative skills were as sophisticated as building techniques. The best examples of Roman art in Leicester are the mosaic pavements which formed the floors of houses and public buildings. Ratae was a remote outpost of the Roman Empire but the displays in Jewry Wall Museum show that it was thought worthy of fine buildings and craftsmanship.

The Jewry Wall site and St Nicholas' Church contain evidence from the first thousand years of the shaping of Leicester. Britain ceased to be part of the Roman Empire in about AD 410 and the centuries that followed left few written records. The Saxon culture, at first pagan and then Christian from about the seventh

ABOVE Arch formed in tile-like Roman brick, Jewry Wall

RIGHT Saxon window opening, Roman bricks used to form arches, St Nicholas' Church

ABOVE FAR RIGHT Theatrical mask from the Blue Boar Lane wall painting, possibly representing the god Dionysus, Roman, Jewry Wall Museum

LOWER FAR RIGHT Vaughan College and Jewry Wall Museum (1960-62) and Jewry Wall site

century AD, gradually became dominant in the Midlands. Fragments in St Nicholas' Church tell something of the later phase in that period.

St Nicholas' Church was built on the site of one of the Roman public buildings. It might have been the seat of the first bishop based in Leicester. To build the church the Saxon masons used materials from the Roman buildings. The clearest evidence of their work is two windows now inside the north wall of the church. The arches over the deep windows are made of the flat, durable Roman brick and echo the design of the openings in the Jewry Wall outside.

Perhaps the most dramatic time in the six centuries after the Roman withdrawal was the occupation of a large part of the East Midlands by the Danes between

RIGHT Jewry Wall and St Nicholas' Church

LOWER RIGHT Nave of St Nicholas' Church, north wall with Saxon windows

the mid-870s and the early tenth century. The Danish contribution to the character of Leicester today is found mainly in street names - Sanvey Gate, Church Gate, Woodgate and Gallowtree Gate - derived from *gata*, the Danish word for road.

Jewry Wall and St Nicholas' Church may tell the story of the beginnings of Leicester but the scene itself is very different from the one left by the Saxons. The church tower was built in the following phase of Leicester's history, by the Normans. And the church was changed and added to later in the Middle Ages and in the nineteenth century. Gravestones in the churchyard beside the bases of Roman columns, recall the lives of past generations in the parish. The site of the Roman baths is now enclosed by Jewry Wall Museum and Vaughan College, designed by the architect Trevor Dannatt and built in 1960-62.

# 3
# *The Normans*

THE NORMANS arrived in Leicester after the Battle of Hastings in 1066, bringing with them French language and culture and building styles from Northern France. They raised the Castle Mound *(Motte)* to a height of about 15 metres and built a wooden stockade *(bailey)* on the top. It must have loomed over the little houses of the Saxons and Danish people as a symbol of the new power of the Norman barons. The top was flattened in the nineteenth century to make a bowling green but the view from Castle Gardens still gives an idea of the former dominance of the motte.

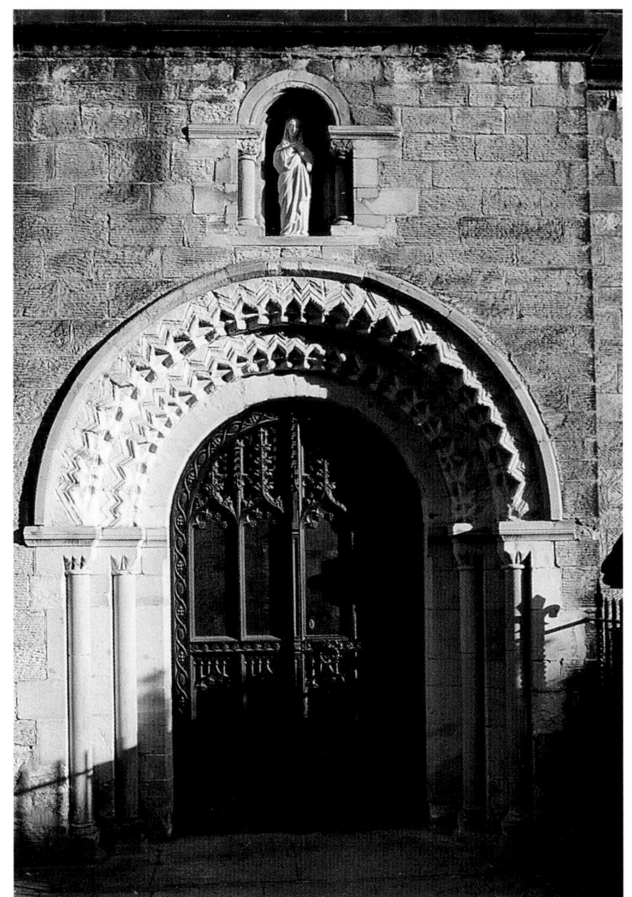

RIGHT Castle Mound: Norman

FACING PAGE
LEFT Castle Hall: brick facade added in late 17th century, central window 18th century

RIGHT Church of St Mary de Castro, north door, late 12th century

Remembrance of
CHARLOTTE
Daughter of
THOMAS
SARAH
who departed this Life

RIGHT St Mary de Castro Churchyard

TOP LEFT Swithland slate roofs in Castle View, note the diminishing courses; the smallest slates laid at the ridge, the largest at the eaves.

TOP CENTRE Castle Hall, Church of St Mary de Castro, and Castle Mound from Castle Gardens

LOWER LEFT Swithland slate headstone in St Mary de Castro Churchyard: note the sharp, calligraphic quality of the incised lines and lettering.

LEFT Norman sedilia, late 12th century, Church of St Mary de Castro

As they established themselves, the Norman lords built up the Castle complex. The Church of St Mary de Castro was begun in about 1107 as a re-foundation of a late Saxon minster. Despite many later changes to the building, much of the architecture which the Normans brought from France is still there. Semicircular arches over windows and doors, decorated with zigzag and other designs, echo styles of the time in France and other continental countries. The church was expanded in the thirteenth century in the Gothic style with its pointed windows and doors. The tower came in 1300. The present spire was built in 1785 and further changes were made by the Victorians.

The materials used to build the church themselves help to form Leicester's character. Light brown local sandstone, soft grey lead roofs, and the crisply chiselled Swithland slate of the gravestones, all add to the special atmosphere of this part of the City.

Building materials are very important in defining the character of particular places. Until the middle of the nineteenth century, when the railways made it cheaper to carry heavy goods around the country, all except the most important buildings were made of materials found close at hand. Swithland slate comes only from the Charnwood Forest area to the north of Leicester. It is used mainly as a roofing material and the distinctive pattern it makes can be seen on houses in Castle View. The individual slates are of different sizes, the smallest being laid at the top of the roof. It also has rougher edges than the more common Welsh slates giving the roof a more rugged appearance. Swithland slate has not been produced for over a hundred years so this important element in the character of Leicester and Leicestershire may gradually be lost.

One of the most impressive parts of the Castle has in the past been rarely seen by most Leicester people and visitors. The Castle Hall, for centuries used as courts, is held by some scholars to be the oldest aisled

ABOVE Castle Hall, 12th century: much restored and altered in later centuries

ABOVE RIGHT Castle House, mid-14th century and 18th century

RIGHT Spire of St Mary de Castro, rebuilt 1785, and lights of Glenfield Road

and bay-divided hall in Europe. It has been much altered, particularly during the sixteenth century and the nineteenth century, but fragments of the work of the carpenters who built the roof for the Norman lords in the middle of the twelfth century are still in place. The brick front to the Castle Hall was added at the end of the seventeenth century.

Later other buildings appeared around the Castle: the fifteenth century gateway, the Georgian Castle House, and small houses from the mid-eighteenth century and later in Castle View.

These buildings have added to the overall picture features like the simply decorated doorways to the houses in Castle View and the grander Georgian doorway and gates to Castle House.

The Castle buildings have survived as a record of the history of Leicester not because past generations valued them for that reason but because they were useful for practical purposes. This has meant that the

buildings have been greatly altered and added to. The care of older buildings, even today, often depends on finding new uses which will provide funds for careful adaptation and maintenance.

TOP LEFT Casting lead sheet at Norman and Underwood Ltd, Freeschool Lane, running the *strickle* over the molten lead just poured over a sand bed: great skill and accurate timing are needed to produce a sheet of the exact thickness required...

ABOVE ...and cutting the lead sheet after casting

LEFT Leadwork on roof of Church of St Mary de Castro: plaque records date of re-roofing (1933) and the names of the Lord Mayor, Town Clerk, Vicar and Churchwardens

# 4
# *The New Work*

THE LIFE OF THE CASTLE continued for several centuries after it was founded by the Normans. It was a home of the Earls and later the Dukes of Lancaster, one of the most powerful families in England, who would have received royalty as guests at Leicester. John O'Gaunt, Duke of Lancaster, who died in 1399, was the father of King Henry IV. After Henry became king the Castle was absorbed into the Crown estates and declined in national importance. But in the mid-fourteenth century Leicester Castle was at the height of its wealth and power and was expanding southwards by the building of the *new work* (Newarke). Three main elements of the Newarke of the Middle Ages survive: the former Trinity Hospital almshouses, the Turret Gateway, and the Magazine Gateway.

Trinity Hospital was founded in 1331 by Henry, Earl of Lancaster and Leicester. The foundation stood on the site in the Newarke until the Hospital moved to a new building next to Newarke Bridge in 1995. Part of the original building, the chapel and hall, remains. This part of the building has Gothic pointed arches, now filled in, on the sides facing Castle Mound and the Newarke. The mediaeval building was much altered in the eighteenth century. The former residential

ABOVE Trinity Hospital: part of remaining 14th century building, much altered in 18th century

ABOVE RIGHT Trinity Hospital:14th century window

FAR RIGHT The Herb Garden and Turret Gateway

FACING PAGE
LEFT Turret Gateway, 15th Century

RIGHT Trinity Hospital: plaque commemorating rebuilding in 1901

part of the Hospital building was designed by the architect R.J. Goodacre in 1901. It was built alongside what was then a new road through the area crossing the river by the Newarke Bridge. The Hospital buildings are now Trinity House, part of De Montfort University.

The Magazine Gateway was built at about the end of the fourteenth century. It too is in the Gothic style but the flattish *four-centred* arches of the main gate openings are characteristic of the development of the style from the late fourteenth century onwards. Between the arches the passage has an impressive *rib-vaulted* ceiling. The Gateway was built for display and as part of the Castle's living space rather than for defence. Inside the building, now the Museum of the Royal Leicestershire Regiment, are two fireplaces, one with a triangular arched head and one with a flattened arch. The name Magazine derives from the use of the building in the Civil War as a store for arms.

Opening-up the City Centre to motor vehicles and improving north-south traffic flow might have

brought advantages to Leicester. But the isolation of the Magazine Gateway in the middle of busy roads, and the loss of the space it stood in, is an example of the enormous destruction that was caused to provide extra convenience for motorists. Since 1995 links between the Newarke and the Magazine Gateway have been improved by the development of Newarke Green by the City and County Councils and De Montfort University. The Newarke Subway, an otherwise hostile place for pedestrians, has been transformed into a work of art using mosaics and ironwork designed by Sue Ridge in 1991-92. It was also made safer by improving security and taking out blind corners.

In the eighteenth century the Newarke remained the select, secluded suburb it had been in the Middle Ages. Building work had not stood still: Wyggeston's Chantry House was built in about 1511 and

TOP The Newarke with the Chantry House, Skeffington House and the Magazine Gateway: Newarke Green laid out in 1995

ABOVE Skeffington House: built c1600 on earlier foundations, much altered and extended in 18th century and c1800, gates and doorway,

RIGHT Magazine Gateway, c1410, fireplace

ABOVE Gateway School: front of 18th century house incorporated into later buildings

ABOVE RIGHT The Newarke: in front of Gateway School

RIGHT Detail of mosaic mural by Sue Ridge 1991-92: Newarke Subway

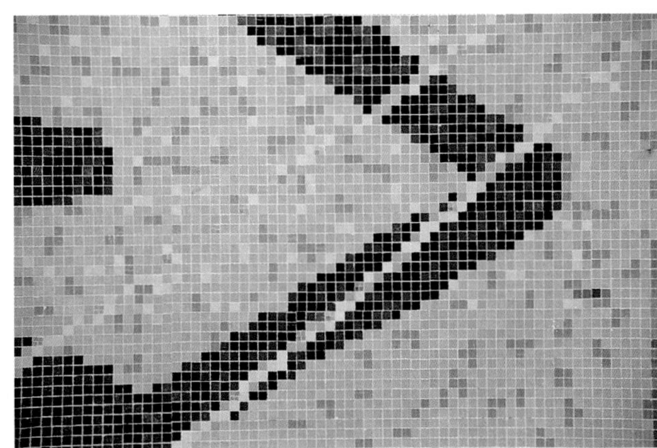

Skeffington House between 1560 and 1583. These two buildings today form Newarke Houses Museum. Skeffington House was greatly altered at the end of the seventeenth century and during the eighteenth. The battlements and Tudor windows are elements of the *Gothick* style: a free, decorative interpretation of mediaeval Gothic used in the late eighteenth and early nineteenth centuries. The elegant front to Gateway School is also a survival of the Georgian Newarke.

Although the area around them has completely changed during their lives the buildings piece together a picture which illustrates important aspects of the character of Leicester. As with the Castle area, building materials are important. The Newarke has a mixture of brick and stone with painted *stucco* (a type of plaster) on Skeffington House. Trees, gardens and the ironwork of railings and gates soften and add detailed quality to the street scene. The former Trinity Hospital combines brick, stone, and slate with fine cast iron rainwater heads.

# 5
# *Church and Guild*

GUILDHALL LANE, once known as Town Hall Lane, contains evidence from several periods of Leicester's history. There were Roman buildings along it and it might have been the route of the Fosse Way, the main road through the Roman town. The Roman and mediaeval street patterns were only loosely related but Guildhall Lane was clearly an important street in the mediaeval town also. Under buildings on the north side there is an undercroft of a Norman merchant's house. For us Guildhall Lane serves to illustrate the contribution made to the City by the guilds and by the

TOP Restored timber studs and plaster infill (Guildhall restoration 1992)

RIGHT Guildhall Lane: gable end of east range and doorway to Guildhall (17th century) and part of Great Hall range (late 14th century)

TOP LEFT Guildhall: 17th century doorway

TOP RIGHT The Guildhall: window in west range, late 15th century

ABOVE St Martin's West

church, two of the most important institutions in the life and politics of the mediaeval town.

The part of the Guildhall alongside Guildhall Lane is the oldest, dating from the middle of the fourteenth century. It was built for the Corpus Christi Guild, a religious association which counted among its members the town's wealthiest and most powerful people. Although there were a number of guildhalls in the mediaeval town, the fifteenth century saw a shift of town government to the Corpus Christi hall.

Most of mediaeval Leicester would have been built in wood. The most common type of building would have had a timber frame with mud and plaster filling in the panels. Most of these timber buildings disappeared in or before the nineteenth century but a few

ABOVE Guildhall: fireplace in Mayor's Parlour, dated 1637 (photo: Leicester Museums Service)

TOP RIGHT Restored timber building at rear of 42 Silver Street

fragments remain, often behind more recent frontages. One example of a mediaeval or later timber building, behind number 42 Silver Street, was restored by the City Council with help from English Heritage in 1992.

The Guildhall stands out in the predominantly brick City of today but in its own time would have been a more than usually grand example among many timber-framed buildings. It grew over several centuries and was adapted and used for a variety of purposes. In 1992-93 a restoration scheme was carried out, helped by English Heritage and supervised by the City Council. The contractors employed by the Council were part of the same tradition of carpentry skills as the original builders. The changes made to the Guildhall throughout its life are elements in the character of the building and provide keys to its history and to the history of the City.

The centuries of use as a civic building have left leaded windows with painted glass, a seventeenth century doorway, and wall paintings. Two elements are particularly impressive. First, the curved cruck trusses that the mid-fourteenth century carpenters raised to support the earliest part of the building, still at the heart of the Guildhall. Secondly, the ornate 1637 fireplace in the Mayor's Parlour: an extravagant piece of craftsmanship from the time of Charles I.

Guildhall: the Great Hall after 1992 restoration

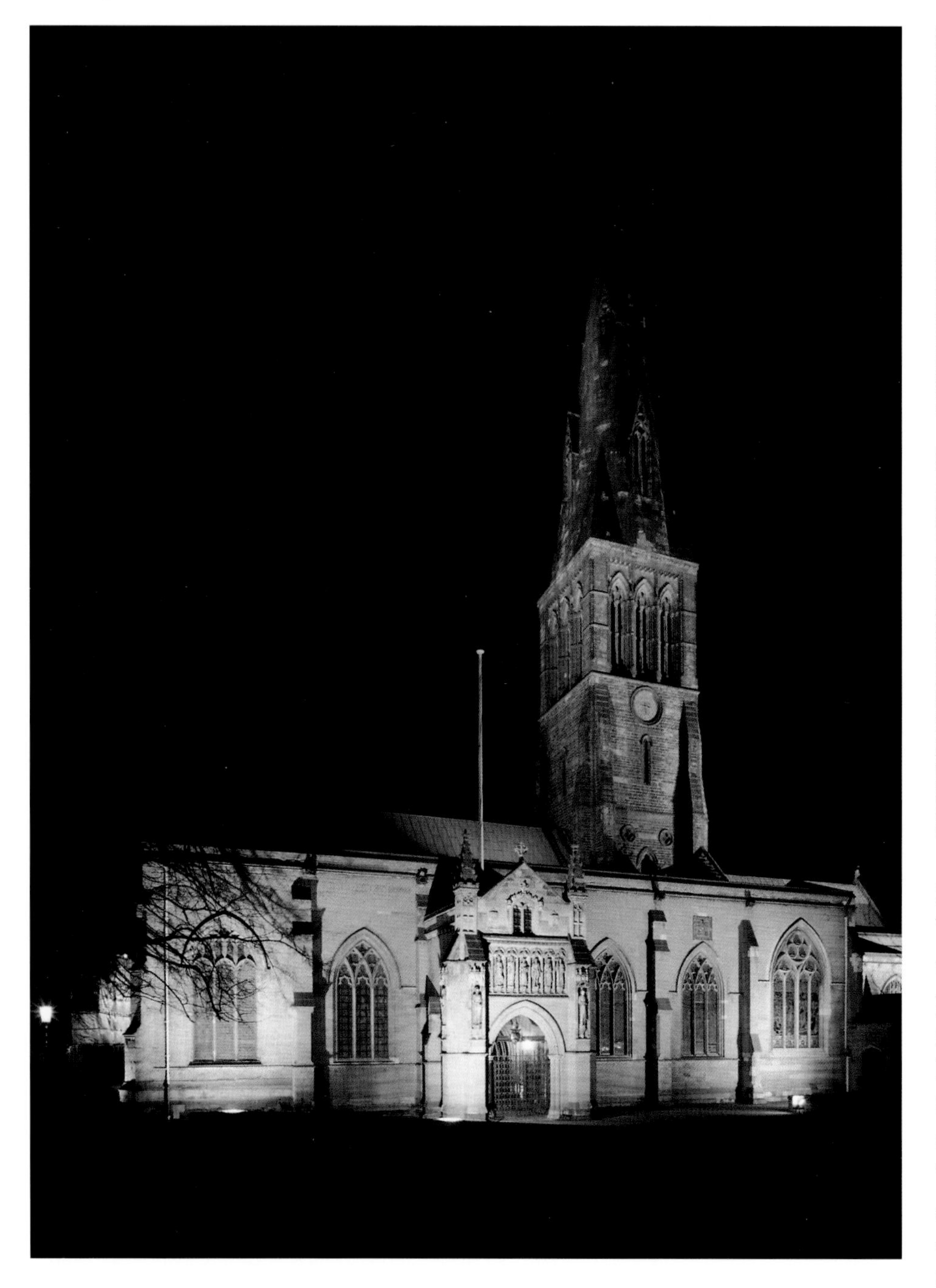

ABOVE St Martin's Cathedral Church: mid 19th century remodelling of mediaeval church

ABOVE RIGHT Cathedral north turret, 19th century

LOWER RIGHT Gates to Cathedral south porch

St Martin's Church, the Cathedral, is a largely Victorian building on the outside. But what is seen today is the re-modelling of the mediaeval church, parts of which remain inside. The Victorian re-modelling was designed by Raphael Brandon, with later contributions from nationally eminent architects G.E. Street and J.L. Pearson. The work was carried out over several decades starting in the 1850s. The nineteenth century Gothic architecture is based on the styles of the Middle Ages when St Martin's was the most important church in a town where life largely revolved around religion. The north turret, with animals carved in stone looming over the narrow street, adds a particularly mediaeval touch.

Georgian and Victorian buildings line Guildhall Lane today and the street has a lively variety of building materials and styles. There is Venetian Gothic from 1868 at the corner of Carts Lane. A group of small

RIGHT Bents Buildings, 1868, Guildhall Lane/Carts Lane

FAR RIGHT 17A Guildhall Lane: early 20th century

LOWER RIGHT 2-8 Guildhall Lane: 18th century

Georgian houses have doors and windows based on Classical proportions derived from the architecture of Ancient Greece and Rome.

In the late nineteenth century and early in the twentieth, some attractive industrial buildings were added. Number 17A is highly individual with its mixture of brick and stone and Gothic details in the windows. In 1990 number 41 Guildhall Lane, an early twentieth century factory building, was converted to offices and its appearance changed by adding tall, timber bay windows. Other factory buildings have also been converted to office or educational use.

TOP LEFT Swithland slates stacked in courses of similar size awaiting re-laying (Guildhall restoration 1992)

LEFT Roofer at work laying Swithland slates on Great Hall (Guildhall restoration 1992)

TOP RIGHT St Martin's East

# 6
# *The Market*

THE MIDDLE AGES also left what many people think of as the heart of Leicester, the Market. Other important institutions of the mediaeval town the Castle, the guilds and the monasteries, have been consigned to history. The churches have lost their mediaeval dominance. The Market still thrives although it is the only remaining example of several which existed in the Middle Ages. The people who came to buy and sell when the Market was founded over seven hundred years ago would recognise only a few of the goods on offer today, but they could still feel at home in the noise and bustle of the Market Place on a Saturday morning.

TOP The Market Place: the space from the Town Hall clock tower

RIGHT The Market: Corn Exchange bridge, 1855, and statue of the Duke of Rutland by Edward Davis, 1851: The Journal *The Builder* commented on the statue in 1851: *His Grace is made to appear positively intoxicated.*

Thirteenth century Leicester people would find little else about the modern Market familiar. Nearly all the buildings around the Market Place are Georgian, Victorian or of the twentieth century. The Market has been roofed only in the twentieth century. But it is to the Middle Ages that we owe the space and the position of the Market Place. The streets called Market Place and Market Place South extend beyond today's Market towards Hotel Street. The buildings between these two streets would have developed from market stalls which gradually established rights and became replaced by permanent structures. This encroachment on the space of market places is common in English towns. Stalls which developed into buildings were usually those of butchers or fishmongers; it is appropriate that these goods are sold in this part of the Market Place, in the indoor Market Centre, today.

ABOVE The Market: a mediaeval institution serving the needs of modern Leicester

RIGHT Pearce and Sons, Market Place: roof timbers of c1500 just visible through second floor windows, gables 17th century, shopfront late 19th/early 20th century

FAR RIGHT
TOP AND BOTTOM
The Market

RIGHT The High Cross, Cheapside: part of a 16th century building placed in Cheapside in 1976

LOWER RIGHT 4 Market Place: gilded lettering

FAR RIGHT Old Fish Market: designed by William Millican 1881

Until 1884 Leicester had another market in Highcross Street. In 1976 a reminder of that other market was moved to the present market place and a small square laid out around it. The project was funded by the Rotary Club of Leicester to mark their sixtieth anniversary. The High Cross was one of the columns of a domed market cross which formed the centrepiece of the market in Highcross Street. There is a cross set into the road where it once stood.

The Corn Exchange, originally a place for dealing in grain, was designed by the architect William Flint and built in 1850. The upper floor, bridge and tower were added by another architect, F.W. Ordish, five years later. The tower, with its upward sweeping lines and decorative work, is a prominent landmark and the bridge brings a touch of Italy to Leicester's Market Place.

Until the Market Centre was opened in 1974, fish was sold in the little cast iron Fish Market on Market Place South. The City Council decided that this building should be kept when the traders moved to the new building and it was converted to shops by Penwise Properties Ltd. in 1978. The Old Fish Market echoes the liveliness of the design of the Corn Exchange in the lettering in the gables and the ironwork supporting the roof.

Pearce's jeweller's shop hides more evidence of the Middle Ages. Behind the seventeenth century gables and the ornate Edwardian shopfront are roof timbers dating from around 1500. This building, like the Guildhall, was the work of the Corpus Christi Guild.

ABOVE LEFT Corn Exchange: 1850 and 1855

ABOVE RIGHT Old Fish Market

RIGHT Fish stalls, Market Centre 1972-5

The Market Centre was built by the City Council in 1973 and gave more hygienic accommodation for the Fish Market and the butchers' stalls that once stood in Cheapside. Inside, the Market Centre has its own atmosphere and colour: the fish stalls especially are one of the sights which any visitor to Leicester should be sure to see. But the building looms massive and solid over the narrow streets and is faced in a hard red brick popular at the time although different in character from the traditional Leicester brick. Perhaps if the Market Centre had been built twenty years later the opportunity would have been taken to knit a building carefully into the pattern and scale of the mediaeval streets rather than impose a powerful new structure upon them.

# 7
# *Mediaeval Manor*

UNTIL WELL INTO the twentieth century Evington was one of a ring of villages separated from Leicester by fields and woods. Like Humberstone, Aylestone, Braunstone, Knighton and Belgrave, it is now within the built-up area of the City but keeps something of its village character. Each of these villages adds something of its own to the varied quality of Leicester.

We can still look out from the village centre of Evington across open countryside and it is in Evington that the modern City has a particularly good record of the village life of the Middle Ages.

To the west of St Denys' Church is a mound surrounded by a deep ditch. This was the property of John de Grey who built a stone manor house on the

Moated site and St Denys' Church, Evington

ABOVE Moated Manor House site, Evington: late 13th/early 14th century

RIGHT Gargoyle, St Denys' Church, Evington

mound in the twelfth century. The moat would have been filled with water but was probably more of a status symbol than a defence. It is many centuries since the building itself was lost but the site is still clearly visible. Nearby are the remains of fishponds which would have supplied food to the manor house. Further away, on Evington Brook, is another earthwork which might have been a dam to serve a water mill providing the manor with flour.

The stone from the manor house was probably taken for building elsewhere. The church is a more durable institution and St Denys', built around the same time as the manor, is another key to the life of the mediaeval village.

Most of St Denys' Church dates from the late thirteenth century or the early fourteenth century. The Gothic style of architecture, with pointed windows and doors, went through changes as it developed over time and had three main phases in its English form. In the nineteenth century historians gave names to the three phases. The first, which was characteristic of the thirteenth century, was called *Early English*; the

second, favoured in most of the fourteenth century, *Decorated*; and the third, from late in the fourteenth century until about 1530, *Perpendicular*. All three forms can be found in churches and other buildings in Leicester but St Denys' illustrates them in a single building. At the west end of the south aisle the window is in the Early English style. It has stone bars or *tracery* forming the shape of the letter Y. An earlier form of the Gothic window, not found at St Denys', had openings simply cut out of a slab of stone. If we move across to the west end of the north aisle the window is a textbook example of the Decorated style.

TOP LEFT TO RIGHT
Windows at St Denys' Church:

South aisle: Early English Y-tracery, 13th century

North aisle: Decorated style window, early 14th century

North aisle: Perpendicular style window, after late 14th century

Chancel East Window: Victorian Decorated style, 1870

RIGHT Mud boundary Wall, St Mary's Churchyard, Humberstone. The mud has been burrowed into by bees. Note also the brick and slate coping and stone base: like a baby a mud wall needs a dry hat and a dry bottom!

It has flowing, intricate, net-like tracery and is covered in small ornaments called *ballflowers*. Moving round to the east end of the north aisle, nearest to Church Road, the window is in the Perpendicular style with the vertical bars running from top to bottom of the window and a square grid of tracery. This window also has a few fragments of mediaeval glass.

Victorian architects revived the Gothic style and the Goddard practice designed the east window at St Denys' as part of a new chancel built in 1867 in the Decorated style.

The church and the manor house would have been the grandest buildings in the village of the Middle Ages and at the centre of village life. But there would have been many other houses and farm buildings. Most of the smaller houses would have been built of materials which could be found close by and these would usually have been wood, straw and mud. These continued to be common materials for smaller buildings for centuries. As late as 1830 the writer and traveller William Cobbett, describing Knighton, wrote of the:

*...miserable sheds in which the labourers reside...look at these hovels, made of mud and straw; bits of glass, or of old off-cast windows, without frames or hinges, frequently but merely stuck in the mud wall*
William Cobbett *Rural Rides.*

These houses have long since been replaced by more permanent structures but, on the north side of St Denys' Churchyard, there is a piece of mud wall illustrating a building type which would once have been common. The mud would have been taken from the nearest supply and bands of different colour

ABOVE AND RIGHT
Shady Lane

FAR RIGHT Figure of St Denys, north aisle St Denys' Church

can be seen. This particular building might have been a farm building or shed when it was built: this would account for the late use of the cheap construction. In 1991 it was incorporated, along with its roof timbers, into an outbuilding of a new private house on the site and is now behind a fence on the edge of the churchyard, not accessible to the public.

Shady Lane was laid out in 1850. Now it appears the most rural of all Leicester's roads. In 1970 a collection of specimen trees was planted by the Corporation on the land next to the Lane to form Evington Arboretum. The 1960s and 1970s saw the loss of many of the older buildings in Evington and great changes to the centre of the village. But the site of the manor house, the church and Shady Lane make a unique contribution to Leicester's character.

The Arboretum and the golf course form part of a *green wedge* which, despite building to the south of Gartree Road and possible interruption by road construction, brings open space from the countryside deep into the built-up area of Leicester.

# PART TWO

98 New Walk

*From the sixteenth through to the early nineteenth century the character of Leicester was that of a county town: a centre for trading, justice and social life. There was a growing industrial base but Leicester remained, by modern standards, a small town surrounded by villages rather than an industrial city. The area covered by the City today was still mostly countryside.*

TOP Great Meeting Unitarian Church, 1708

ABOVE Aylestone Hall, late-mediaeval - 17th century - 18th century

# 8
# *Renaissance*

THE SIXTEENTH and seventeenth centuries have left few contributions to Leicester's modern character. Many buildings were victims of the prosperity of the Victorian town. Skeffington House and Wyggeston's Chantry House in the Newarke, the Free Grammar School in Highcross Street, the Mayor's Parlour and Town Library at the Guildhall, Cavendish House in Abbey Park, and parts of Aylestone Hall and Knighton Hall are among the scarce fragments of built evidence of the life of Leicester in those centuries. This is not to say that Leicester stood still. The sixteenth and seventeenth centuries brought radical change here as elsewhere, removing much of the fabric of mediaeval society.

Changes which affected Leicester were largely a reflection of national events. The Abbey and other monasteries were dissolved and destroyed. The power of the guilds was abolished. The town was ravaged by plagues and by the Civil War. But there were advances like the foundation of the Grammar School and the Town Library. The town was granted its first charter of incorporation in 1589: this was an important step in the emergence of local government, recognising the right of the Corporation to hold property for the first time.

The Leicestershire historian John Nichols recorded an event which was to have the most profound effect on Leicester of anything before the twentieth century. In 1680, he wrote:

*Alsop, a Northamptonshire man, came to Leicester and resided in the Parish of All Saints at or near the North-gate-way, where he followed the occupation of stocking maker, being the only person of that trade in Leicester.*

John Nichols *The History and Antiquities of the County of Leicester*

Although the industry developed slowly, knitting and knitting machines were to be the force which transformed Leicester into an industrial city.

There was another change which had a critical effect on Leicester's architectural character: the use of red brick. Brick had been used by the Romans but was then neglected throughout the country until the late fifteenth century. Kirby Muxloe Castle had been built in brick in the 1480s and Bradgate House followed in the 1490s. In Leicester, the brick section of the Abbey boundary wall along St Margaret's Way was built by Abbot Penny in about 1500. (Abbot Penny's Wall will be described in Chapter 20.) In 1695 the front of the Castle Hall was built in brick and there may have been other brick buildings, now lost, by the end of the seventeenth century. A few years later, in 1708, Great Meeting Chapel in East Bond Street was built: it is Leicester's earliest surviving building constructed all in brick.

Red brick is too easily dismissed as dull and commonplace. Until the railways allowed building materials to be moved cheaply around the country, brick was often the local building material closest to hand in areas where there were local supplies of clay. Variations in the nature of clays around the country and in the techniques of firing them produce many different brick types, each one characteristic of the area from which it comes. Even red bricks vary between different locations. The Leicester red brick, from which much of the Victorian town was built, has an attractive orange tint. In other cities the local red brick may be tinted pink or brown.

After the Great Meeting Chapel, the next surviving brick building in Leicester was Belgrave Hall, which was completed in about 1715. Here the bricklayer mixed red and brown bricks in a chequer pattern. Making patterns in brickwork using different coloured bricks goes back to Kirby Muxloe Castle and Abbot Penny's Wall, where the brick *diaper* patterns are more complex, and was often a feature of sixteenth and seventeenth century brickwork. The masons, turning their hand to bricklaying, were quick to use the decorative potential of what for them was a new material. The darker bricks are usually those fired at the top of the kiln where the heat is fiercest and produces a dark, glassy finish.

Another special feature of Belgrave Hall is the lead rainwater heads, tanks, and other fittings for collecting

Belgrave Hall: brick, lead and iron

rainwater. On the rainwater heads in particular the lead was cast by the plumbers into intricate patterns based on the initials and arms of the Cradock family who had the Hall built. The soft grey colour of the lead complements the red and blue of the brick. There are other examples of craftsmanship in lead in the statues and rainwater butt in the garden. For the front of the Hall, the blacksmith made delicate wrought iron gates and railings.

The style chosen for Belgrave Hall was rather plain. The windows and doorways are designed to Classical proportions and there is some decoration around the front door. Belgrave House, on the other side of Church Road, is a more elaborate Classical building of 1776. The main house is large and finely proportioned with an arched centre bay and little decorated

FACING PAGE
TOP Lead rainwater pipes and hopper head, Belgrave Hall

LOWER RIGHT Belgrave Gardens gatepier

LOWER LEFT
Belgrave Hall, 1710

TOP Belgrave House, 1776

LEFT Stable block at Belgrave Hall, 1710

ABOVE Lead rainwater tank, Belgrave Hall

TOP AND ABOVE Belgrave Hall Garden

RIGHT Belgrave Hall Garden: part of monument to Edward Holdsworth, 1764, from Gopsall Hall

RIGHT Belgrave Hall Garden

TOP CENTRE Belgrave Gardens: left to right - Belgrave Hall, Belgrave House, St Peter's Church (Norman and later), Belgrave House Stables

wings at the sides, all in red brick. Both Belgrave House and Belgrave Hall have ranges of stables which are simpler in their design and decoration but still intended to impress passers-by and visitors as signs of their owners' wealth and prestige.

The garden at the back of Belgrave House is now a public park. Its most interesting features are the gatepiers at the entrance from Church Road, built early in the nineteenth century, with their mysterious male figures on the inside faces.

Belgrave Hall garden remains as one of the pleasantest places in the City. It can be reached only through the Hall and its high walls give it a feeling of secrecy and seclusion. Among the many wonderful plants the twisted shapes of the mulberry trees contrast with the smoother sculpted forms of the statues.

As well as monumental buildings and broad highways a city needs the variety provided by quiet and hidden places. Belgrave Hall and Belgrave House, grouped with their outbuildings around St Peter's Church, give this part of Leicester an area of tranquillity. They also illustrate important points about the quality of the City as it developed in the eighteenth century.

TOP LEFT AND RIGHT Belgrave Hall Garden

LEFT Belgrave Gardens

FACING PAGE One of Leicester's best street views: the Cathedral tower and spire from New Street

# 9
# *Georgian Town*

BY THE MIDDLE of the eighteenth century red brick was firmly established as the favoured building material in Leicester. New Street, laid out in the middle of the century on land which had been part of the estate of the Greyfriars, was built mainly in red brick. Most of the buildings in the street, even those from after the eighteenth century, are built to a common set of Classical proportions and in a similar style. The harmony which these rules give to the street is characteristic of Georgian Classical architecture, but the rules allow for rich variety of detail.

Before looking at the details of the buildings it is worth considering the overall qualities of the street. In Georgian cities like Bath or the Edinburgh New Town, streets and squares were laid out in regular patterns. At the ends of important streets there is often a prominent building to hold the attention. New Street, on the other hand, seems to have been built to an irregular line, perhaps a property boundary or a ditch, set out long before the street was built. The narrowness of the street and the bend in the middle give New Street its own quality. Walking along the street, the views at either end are held back until the corner is turned. At the southern end the view is closed by another Georgian building on Friar Lane. To the north, one of the best street views in Leicester, is the Cathedral tower and spire dwarfing the buildings around.

Doors and windows are very important features of Georgian buildings. The builders of the houses in New Street understood the value of good proportions and had a knowledge of appropriate fittings and finishes and of how to make them. The doorway at number 11 has Classical columns forming a porch, built in stone and rebuilt by craftsmen in 1988 after

RIGHT New Street looking south

BOTTOM LEFT TO RIGHT
11 New Street, 18th century: note the windows set nearly flush with the brickwork

8 New Street: windows recessed into brickwork

2 New Street: early 20th century door echoing 18th century style

15 New Street: 1930s interpretation of a Georgian doorway

Doorway, 11 New Street, 18th century

the building had been hit by a passing lorry. At 12 and 14 New Street the doorways are much simpler and made in wood; the centre doorway has glazing in the eighteenth century Gothick style with glazing bars forming little pointed arches.

The windows at number 11 are also worth noting. They are fitted almost flush with the front wall, with woodwork containing the weights which balance the window, exposed on the face of the wall. Towards the end of the eighteenth century it was more common to fit windows a few inches back from the face of the wall with the sash weights hung behind the brickwork to show a slimmer timber surround. Numbers 4 to 8 New Street provide an example of this detail which was intended to make it harder for fire to spread across the front of the building. Setting the window back in a recess also changes the character by introducing extra shadow. These differences tell a story about the development of the City and bring variety to the pattern of the street scene.

The nineteenth and twentieth centuries brought changes to New Street but did not spoil its Georgian character. Stone-fronted buildings at numbers 3 and 5 echo their neighbours in the street without copying them. A 1930s brick building at number 15 fits in with others nearby while introducing a very individual note in the pattern of the metal windows on the ground floor. On the skyline is a craggy collection of nineteenth century chimney pots.

Around the corner from New Street, Friar Lane is broader and the houses are larger. It is worth remembering that buildings in both streets were designed to be lived in although they changed to office use. The grandest of all the houses in Friar Lane, number 17, was a residence until 1903. Built in about 1750 as a town house for the Herrick family, it was not meant to be modest. The doorway has a big triangular *pediment* over it, and above that are a *Venetian window* (in three parts with an arched centre section) and a *Diocletian window* (semicircular with two vertical

ABOVE 18th century townhouses in Friar Lane: Number 17 (c1750) on the right

TOP RIGHT 17 Friar Lane, central bay

BOTTOM RIGHT Doorway, 27 Friar Lane, 18th century

divisions). All these have carved stone surrounds and the other windows have big keystones.

Around the country wealthy merchants and professional people were building themselves large townhouses and 17 Friar Lane can stand comparison with any of them. We can be grateful to the Herricks for displaying their wealth by their choice of building, and to later generations who have ensured that 17 Friar Lane has remained and been looked after, at least on the outside. It is one of Leicester's finest Georgian buildings and helps to show that the nucleus of the City's character was established well before the Victorian growth which now appears dominant.

# 10
# *Country Estate*

BRAUNSTONE HALL was built in 1775 by the Winstanley family, lords of the manor and the main landowners in the village of Braunstone. In many ways the Hall resembles town houses like 17 Friar Lane. It is built in similar materials and has similar Classical proportions and decoration. But, while the Friar Lane houses were lived in by wealthy merchants and professional people or were used as town houses by landed families, Braunstone Hall was the centre of a country estate passed on through the Winstanley family from generation to generation.

Braunstone Hall, approach to front of house

ABOVE Braunstone Hall, front elevation

FAR RIGHT Stable Block, Braunstone Hall, 18th century

RIGHT Butressed garden wall, Braunstone Hall

FACING PAGE

TOP LEFT Braunstone Hall Garden

BOTTOM LEFT AND TOP RIGHT Cressida Place

LOWER RIGHT School and Schoolhouse, 1868, Main Street, Braunstone

As country houses go, Braunstone Hall is fairly unassuming. It was not designed by one of the many fashionable country house architects of the day but by local builder and Leicester politician, William Oldham. He used red brick and Swithland slate, common local materials. The central doorway and windows are emphasised just as they are at 17 Friar Lane. Here they are set in an arched recess reaching up to the top of the facade. The Hall has a slightly less elaborate frontage to the Park at the back and, inside, Classical columns in the entrance hall (probably added in the early twentieth century) and an elegant staircase. Building has always been a dangerous occupation and the building records show that a stonemason and a labourer were killed in the construction of Braunstone Hall.

Around the Hall the Winstanleys had a Park laid out with a lake and gardens. As a wealthy family they had horses and carriages which were kept in the stable block next to the house. These buildings did not share the refinement of the house and were more like farm buildings, but they were still carefully designed, with fine brickwork arches and decoration at the eaves. The walled garden, restored and beautifully planted by the City Council, once contained fruit trees, serving the household both as a source of food and as a place to stroll.

There are reminders of the Winstanleys in the village also. They commissioned one of the most famous of Victorian architects, William Butterfield, to design cottages for estate workers at Cressida Place and in Main Street. Both groups of cottages were built in 1859. Butterfield modelled the houses on traditional buildings and used local materials but their design has a deliberate, thought-out quality which suggests that it was the work of an architect. The parsonage, built in 1864, and the village school of 1867, were paid for by the Winstanleys.

Braunstone was greatly changed in the 1930s when the Winstanley estate was bought by the Corporation, partly as land for new housing. The Winstanleys' park and buildings came to serve people from the crowded centre of Leicester. The Hall was turned into a school and the gardens and the stable block form part of the modern Braunstone Park.

# 11
# *Nineteenth Century*

IN 1801 LEICESTER was a market town with a population of 17,000; by 1901 it had become an industrial city and home to 211,000 people. The built-up area had grown accordingly and the administrative boundaries of the Borough were extended in 1836 and in 1891. National fashions in architecture changed greatly during the course of the nineteenth century and the development of Leicester reflects all these changes, just as it reflects the national changes in transport, industry and the way in which cities were governed.

TOP City Rooms: one of a series of paintings by R. R. Reinagle in the Ballroom

RIGHT City Rooms, 1790s, front elevation

FACING PAGE
LEFT *The Comic Muse:* one of the statues by J. C. Rossi and J. Bingley on the front elevation of City Rooms

RIGHT *The Leicester Seamstress* by James Butler, 1990

The City Rooms (previously County Rooms) were designed as a hotel by the architect John Johnson. The front was in stone, an indication of the building's importance, and decorated with statues and relief panels. On the ground floor the stonework is *rusticated*: the joints are cut out to give the building a strong, solid appearance. In her guidebook to Leicester written in 1804, author Susanna Watts describes the hotel as *the first modern architectural ornament of the town*. The big first floor windows light the ballroom which would have been the scene of social events at the time of the races or the assizes. It is still the most elegant room in Leicester.

John Johnson built his hotel between 1792 and 1800 and it was extended towards the Market Place in 1817.

TOP City Rooms, the Ballroom

FAR RIGHT City Rooms, railings and rusticated stonework

The extension, later the County Fire Offices, is attractive in its own right. It is Classical in style but is different from the houses in Friar Lane or from City Rooms itself. It is built in brick covered in stucco to give a smooth surface. Around the windows and the door the stucco is built out to look bold and chunky. At the top a big cornice projects to give the building further weight. The roof is gently-sloped and invisible from the street.

The early twentieth century was kind to this corner of the City Centre. The pub, whose original name is the Saracen's Head, was designed by the architects

ABOVE Saracen's Head pub, 1901

TOP RIGHT Market Place South

LOWER FAR RIGHT County Fire Offices, 1817-18, designed as an extension to the building now called City Rooms, probably by Joshua Harrison

RIGHT Saracen's Head, lead rainwater spout

Stockdale Harrison and Sons in 1901. It is one of Leicester's best buildings in the Arts and Crafts style fashionable at that time, a style borrowed from the architecture of cottages and simple buildings of the past. Local red brick was used with patterns in blue brick and the building was roofed in Swithland slate. While the architects of buildings like City Rooms and the hotel extension had hidden the roof, here, with the big brick chimney stack, the roof is the most prominent feature of the building. Water drains through a fearsome spout in the shape of a dragon's head.

In the 1970s the area outside City Rooms was made into a paved space free of traffic. The sculpture *the Leicester Seamstress* by James Butler was placed there by the City Council in 1990. In other ways the area has not fared well. The Theatre Royal was demolished in the late 1950s and the site redeveloped for offices. The high, blank side wall dominates the view down Market Place South. The ground floor windows of the extension to the old hotel have been made bigger, changing the balance of its Classical proportions.

# 12
# *New Walk*

IN NEW WALK, Leicester has something unmatched anywhere else in Britain: a promenade designed for walking which has remained all but free of invasion by motor traffic throughout its two-hundred year history. When the Corporation first laid out the Walk in 1785, the town's freemen had long-established grazing rights on the Southfields and New Walk was the Corporation's

New Walk and De Montfort Square, terrace on north side c1850

RIGHT New Walk, junction with King Street

BELOW Upper New Walk, near junction with Granville Road

way of encroaching on this land with the eventual aim of building on it. The freemen's rights were finally given up in 1804. When Susanna Watts described it in her *A Walk through Leicester* in that year, New Walk was still a path through open fields. At one end was the town and, at the other, the racecourse on the land which now forms Victoria Park. The Walk afforded views of Aylestone and Narborough as well as the church spires of the town.

New Walk became a very select area to live in and by the end of the nineteenth century was almost completely built-up. But the key to its character is that it is a park rather than just a collection of buildings. Miss Watts noted two important things about New Walk: it is on a hill and it is not straight. This means that anyone walking along it is faced with stretches where they can see far ahead and others where a curve or a slope holds back the view of the next part of the Walk. Trees bring seasonal changes to the character of New Walk and they

attract squirrels, songbirds and the occasional tawny owl. As the Southfields developed, open spaces were left along the west side of the Walk: Museum Square, De Montfort Square, and the Oval. These, together with the open areas at each end of New Walk, help to prevent it being just a corridor: enclosed stretches alternate with open areas, each space of a different size and with its own atmosphere. De Montfort Square is large and surrounded by buildings. Museum Square and the Oval are built up also but they are smaller and dominated by trees giving them more intimacy. It is variety which makes a stroll along New Walk so delightful: changing views, different spaces, and the changes through the year in the plant and animal life of the Walk. But buildings are important, both in themselves and in giving New Walk a shape.

Holy Cross Chapel, built in 1818, was the first building on New Walk although its main frontage was on Wellington Street. Further building soon followed but between King Street and the Museum most of the houses are in variations on Classical styles. The Corporation insisted that buildings should be set back ten yards from the Walk to prevent it being hemmed-in. Numbers 7-17, by Flint and Wickes of 1852, are in brick with chunky window and door surrounds. They contrast with 19-21, built after 1844, which are faced in stucco and more delicate in their proportions and in the design of items like windows. Next to these are two smaller houses built about 1828. They are even more refined with deep overhanging eaves and curved bow windows.

On the opposite side were once similar houses dating from the 1820s. Now there is a concrete 1970s office block designed by the J. Seymour Harris Partnership of Birmingham. The architects tried to echo something of the other buildings in New Walk by providing a series of vertical bays along the front to the Walk, but the building now seems a harsh addition to an elegant thoroughfare.

RIGHT 19-21 New Walk, pre-1844, to the right Numbers 7-17, 1852

UPPER RIGHT The Oval

FACING PAGE
UPPER LEFT Cast iron parish boundary marker, the Oval

LEFT The Oval: houses of 1850s and 1860s

LOWER LEFT Cricket at the Oval

LEFT *Anthemion* and *palmette* decoration in ironwork, 62-64 New Walk

CENTRE The Museum and 70 New Walk (early nineteenth century)

BELOW LEFT 23-25 New Walk: late 1820s/1830s

BELOW RIGHT 62-64 New Walk, before 1828: note *Greek Key* decoration, *anthemion* capital and Egyptian chimney pots

ABOVE RIGHT The Museum, built as a school in 1836

Some of the houses facing Museum Square have decoration showing the influence of the architecture of Ancient Greece: the square *Greek Key* motif which runs around the top of the frontage of the houses and the *anthemion* (honeysuckle) in the ironwork. The Greek Revival started to make itself felt in English architecture in the later eighteenth century after two intrepid British architects, James Stuart and Nicholas Revett, made the then dangerous journey to Greece and later published their drawings of Greek antiquities. The houses facing Museum Square also have chimney pots derived from ancient Egyptian architecture.

The Museum, originally built as a school in 1836, is one of the main landmarks of New Walk. The scale and plainness of its big Classical portico reflect the serious sense of purpose of the Nonconformists for whose children the school was built. It was designed by Joseph Hansom, whose name is best remembered as the designer of the Hansom Cab, but whose finest work as an architect includes Birmingham Town Hall. In Leicester Hansom also designed the 'Pork Pie Chapel' in Belvoir Street. Opposite the museum is a group of houses from the 1820s or 1830s.

In the 1970s Waterloo Way was driven through the line of New Walk. Houses were knocked down to make way for the road but something of the special quality of the Walk was safeguarded by running the new road through a big cutting under the promenade.

Building also took place before the 1840s around De Montfort Square. Numbers 98-104 introduce a rather unusual greyish red brick into New Walk. The houses in this terrace are mostly quite plain but they have columns at the doorways and delicate curved glazing bars

RIGHT Upper New Walk, near junction with Granville Road: houses of 1877 and 1889

TOP LEFT TO RIGHT
De Montfort Square, c1850

Lamp standard in Museum Square: the base is an upturned Corinthian capital

74-80 New Walk, c1836

Museum Square, 1852

in the fanlights over the doors. In the 1870s there was a fashion for bay windows which must have been like more recent fashions for artificial stone cladding or plastic windows and doors. This terrace did not escape the bay window craze and they were built onto several houses adding a rather clumsy element to the simple original design. The fine terrace by William Flint on the north side of De Montfort Square has been converted by the City Council to provide sheltered flats for elderly people. It is an example of a *palace front*: a terrace designed to look like a single grand house with clearly emphasised centre and end bays.

Next to De Montfort Street is the tall, slim spire of St Stephen's United Reformed Church, another of the main landmarks on New Walk. It was designed by A.R.G. Fenning and originally built on London Road. The church was moved to make way for the Station and rebuilt on New Walk in the 1890s, bringing stone into the pattern of brick and stucco. The rebuilt church was smaller than the original and there was enough stone to front the manse next door on De Montfort Street. In the 1860s local builder William Rushin built a series of paired houses between De Montfort Street and University Road. By this time the Classical styles of the earlier houses in New Walk were unfashionable but Rushin carried them on using brick and stone, either through innate conservatism or to maintain the mood already established. The trees and decorative railings carry the view round the curve of New Walk to University Road. The Oval, because of its shape and woodland character, is the most distinctive of the open spaces along New Walk. Inside the railings are two cast iron boundary markers separating the historic parishes of St Mary's and St Margaret's.

Beyond University Road, in Upper New Walk, the gradient is steeper and there is a very different set of buildings. They were built in the 1880s and the feeling

RIGHT 100-102 New Walk: pre-1844 with later bays

LOWER RIGHT 146-152 Upper New Walk, 1884-88

of calmness and regularity of the Classical buildings has disappeared. Stockdale Harrison, the architect of 2 University Road and 146-154 Upper New Walk, freely mixed timber framing, gables, a turret, wooden balconies, bay windows, decorated doorways, brick, lead, woodwork, and stone. The most striking difference between these houses and those nearer the City Centre is the pattern of the roofs. On the Classical houses the eaves line is usually straight with the roof and chimneys rising behind. Here it leaps up and down, with gables and turrets topped by *finials*, spikes of lead or terracotta, and a terracotta dragon. A similarly dramatic group turns the corner at the end of New Walk, taking it into Granville Road.

At the points where New Walk crosses De Montfort Street and Waterloo Way, and at the junction with King Street, there are cast iron throwover arches with lanterns. They have lotus leaf decoration derived from the architecture and art of ancient Egypt. These columns were cast in the Leicester foundry of S. Wright and can be found in streets around the City. Other street lamps have climbing plants cast into their iron shafts: a design originally imported from Paris. The

RIGHT AND FAR RIGHT 154 Upper New Walk, 1888

FACING PAGE
TOP The Crescent and Holy Trinity Church

BOTTOM The Crescent, 1826-28, central doorways

lamps provide a theme which ties the lower end of New Walk together. Outside the Museum is a particularly elaborate street lamp with an upturned capital of a Classical column as its base.

The twentieth century has made its contributions to New Walk. It has changed from a mainly residential area and today most of the properties are used as offices. Some new buildings, like the private detached house built in the early 1980s at 155 Upper New Walk, respect its character. Others have been deliberately designed to match the older buildings around them. But New Walk is a special part of the City and buildings like the red-brick office block at 16 West Walk and Salisbury House at the corner of Salisbury Road, make no concessions to its character at all. The surface of New Walk itself is also a problem. It is regularly dug up to get access to cables for telephones, electricity and TV, and to gas and water mains. The patches of replacement tarmac give the surface a perpetually unfinished appearance.

Money from the City Council and English Heritage is funding a programme of repairs to buildings, restoration of boundary walls and railings, better lighting and other improvements.

Despite the problems and the pressures for change, New Walk remains a delight. The Corporation in 1785 may have had ulterior motives for making the Walk in the first place, but it gave us something to treasure and enjoy - and provided a glimpse of what cities could be like if we chose to make them so.

# 13
# *Expansion*

LEICESTER was more fortunate than many other towns in the early nineteenth century in being able to overcome relatively easily the legal difficulties which might have prevented expansion beyond the mediaeval core of the town. Much of the housing which resulted from this expansion would not have appeared desirable by today's standards, but it was thought healthy and spacious at the time. By contrast, Nottingham was a beautiful town at the beginning of the eighteenth century but was swamped by slum housing when industrial and population growth took place without an adequate supply of land.

We have seen that the laying-out of New Walk in 1785 was the first step in encroaching on the fields to the south of Leicester. The legal process which resulted in the Corporation building on the Southfields was not completed until 1811. Then the local authority quickly began laying out streets in a piece of early town planning. King Street was formed in 1811 to 1813, Wellington Street in 1812, and Princess Road in 1815.

Developing the Southfields was a profitable business for the Corporation and its individual members, and it produced some fine buildings. One of the earliest was the Crescent on King Street, designed by William Firmadge in 1826. He used red brick and the building is generally quite plain. Its contribution to the street scene is in its shape, curving elegantly back from the street frontage behind the row of horse chestnut trees which now lines the pavement. The main decorative feature is supplied by the blacksmith who made the delicate ironwork of the porch and balcony framing the central doorway.

RIGHT Upper King Street and Crescent Cottages, 1830s

BOTTOM LEFT Crescent Cottages, 1836

BOTTOM RIGHT Holy Trinity Church, built 1838 - remodelled 1871

The revival of Gothic architecture in the nineteenth century was associated particularly with High Church Anglicanism and Catholicism and was much slower to become popular in Nonconformist Leicester than in some other towns. When it was first built in 1838, Holy Trinity Church was a Classical landmark to catch the eye at the end of King Street and to match the style of the buildings around it. But the church was completely remodelled in 1871 by the nationally known architect S.S. Teulon. There are still traces of the old church but Teulon was known for his highly individual style of Gothic architecture. He went much further than simply transposing the styles of the Middle Ages to the nineteenth century and his buildings were controversial in their own time. The bold design of Holy Trinity, emphasised by the use of dark purple brick and white stone, is perhaps heavy-handed but appears very striking and different from that of any other church in Leicester.

In the same year that the original church appeared, Crescent Cottages were built on the other side of Regent Road. Just as the church is an important feature of the street because it stands at the end of a vista along King Street, Crescent Cottages are important because they are at a corner, with the curved central bay leading the eye round from Regent Road into King Street.

The Cottages form part of a group with buildings on the opposite side of Regent Road and running the length of Upper King Street. This corner of the City looks more like a Regency spa town, such as Cheltenham or Leamington, than red-brick Leicester. The most obvious thing which makes the buildings so different is the smooth stucco outer covering to the brickwork. Cornices and window surrounds stand proud of the face of the wall and are made bolder by painting in a colour different from the background. Like some of the houses in New Walk these buildings have the *anthemion* (honeysuckle) decoration moulded into the stucco.

ABOVE Newtown Street / Regent Road junction, houses 1830s/1840s

TOP RIGHT Entrance to Holy Trinity Church, Upper King Street, 1986

MIDDLE RIGHT 10 Newtown Street, 1830s/1840s

BOTTOM RIGHT Railings, Regent Road / King Street junction

The architect of Crescent Cottages and some of the houses nearby was probably William Flint who was well-versed in the styles made popular by the Greek Revival. He designed the Baptist Church in Charles Street in 1830 with columns of the Greek Doric order and the anthemion decoration in the stucco and in the ironwork of the gates.

Today, most of the Greek Revival houses in King Street and Upper King Street have been converted to offices. Crescent Cottages, with its railings matching the colour scheme of the building, is well looked after and is one of the City's most attractive landmarks. The Church has a modern entrance onto Upper King Street, as much of its own time as Teulon's Gothic remodelling was in its day.

The development of the Southfields continued on a formal grid pattern of streets between Regent Road and Lancaster Road through into the 1870s. There are some very distinctive groups like the cottages at 77 to 95 Regent Road, built as an isolated terrace in 1841, and the much later houses nearby on West Street. The building of the Prison, designed by William Parsons as the County Gaol in 1828, might have been expected to reduce the popularity of the Southfields but housing continued to develop around its massive brick boundary walls. The walls of the Prison, simple and powerful, are almost more im-

pressive than its sham-castle gatehouse in Derbyshire sandstone. The coming of the railway to the Southfields in 1839 also did little long term damage to its success as a residential area.

The houses are mainly in red brick with slate roofs but this superficial similarity hides great variety of detail which gives clues as to the varying ages of the properties which developed plot by plot over several decades. 10 and 12 Newtown Street are particularly impressive with their bold, simple Classical design, probably from the 1830s.

In the 1970s and 1980s the area benefited greatly from the City Council's Housing Renewal Strategy which gave new life to the houses and strengthened the community life of the Southfields as it did in many other parts of the inner city. This dramatic story will be described in more detail in Chapter 17.

TOP Lancaster Road, houses probably 1850s/1870s, and Prison boundary wall, 1828

ABOVE LEFT West Street: probably 1860s/1870s

ABOVE RIGHT Sham-castle gatehouse to HM Prison, Welford Road, 1828: note the portcullis carved in stone over the entrance arch

UPPER RIGHT 77-95 Regent Road, 1841

LOWER RIGHT Charles Street Baptist Church, 1830: Greek Revival decoration on gates and piers and *Greek Doric* columns supporting the porch

# PART THREE

Midland Bank Granby Street

*The Victorian town was marked by rampant energy and rapid expansion. This pace of growth brought problems to which the Victorians tried to find solutions. Many of Leicester's streets and buildings appeared in the period between 1840 and 1914. The many parallel currents in the Victorian development of Leicester have prompted a looser arrangement of chapters than the previous steady, chronological sequence.*

# 14
# *Industry*

NINETEENTH-CENTURY Leicester was not a resort town nor primarily a trading centre. The town was built by the skills of its people and the enterprise of its industrialists in making things and selling them. The product for which Leicester is best known, hosiery, was made mainly in the homes of the framework knitters themselves until the middle of the century. Other industries, including those connected with hosiery, became factory-based much earlier.

Friars' Mills were built around the turn of the eighteenth and nineteenth centuries. The factory originally

UPPER RIGHT Former Pex factory 1840-1850

RIGHT Friars' Mills, late 18th/early 19th century, and Pex Factory, 1840-1850, (Friars' Mills Engine House mid-late 19th century)

Friars' Mills

made worsted thread. Donisthorpe and Co. have been on the site since the 1860s, although they now make very different products by modern processes. The factory is a Classical building in red brick. The centre is emphasised by raising the roof to form a gable echoing the pediment on buildings like 17 Friar Lane. The ibex weather vane displayed the company's trade mark in a charming and effective way. Generations of Leicester people have worked here and in the mid-1980s Donisthorpes refurbished the best of the old buildings and modernised the complex to equip it for many more years of modern industrial production. The work was supported by a loan made by the City Council and central government under the scheme then known as Urban Development Grant.

Just on the other side of West Bridge is another prominent factory building, West Bridge Mills, also built for producing worsted. It was designed in about 1850 by William Flint for John Whitmore and Sons but for many years was the premises of Pex Ltd. Flint's building has a chunky appearance with big overhanging eaves. It shows the influence of Italian architecture in the tower which is modelled on a *campanile* or bell tower.

The Pex site, now called West Bridge Place, is one of the focal points of Leicester's City Challenge programme which brings in central government funding to encourage development and improvements in the inner city. The main factory building, with a new extension, provides modern offices at the centre of a scheme that will also include a pub, cafe and workshops. The new complex will be linked to Castle Gardens via a new footbridge. Like Donisthorpes, Pex shows that historic buildings often have built-in qualities of flexibility that enable them to provide for modern needs: a lesson that could be much better learnt by the development industry.

Opposite the Pex development is a feature which often attracts the attention of visitors to Leicester: the 'hole in the wall' by West Bridge. The mermaids originally swam further from the water at the Wholesale Market, which stood in Halford Street until the late 1960s. Other market buildings around the country have been given lively new uses but the Halford Street buildings were knocked down to make way for a dreary office block and car park. The mermaid panels are signed by the terracotta artist William J. Neatby of the Royal Doulton factory in London and were made in 1900. The Turkey Cafe in Granby Street (Chapter 18) is another example of Neatby's work.

Close to the river, less than half a mile to the south, a cluster of fine industrial buildings represents a later stage in Leicester's industrial development. One of the City's most distinctive factories stands in Henshaw Street. The saw-tooth silhouette of the roof and the large expanses of glass distinguish the former Luke Turner & Co elastic webbing factory from many of its neighbours. This distinctiveness is due partly to its peculiar iron-frame construction, very early for 1893 when the factory was built. Perhaps the building also owes its individuality to the origin of its design in north-west England. There are many examples of the work of the architects Stott and Sons in Manchester and Oldham but this is their only building in Leicester.

Next to the Luke Turner works is the former hosiery factory of Harrison & Hayes with its main frontage to Gateway Street. This building is less distinctive structurally than its neighbour but its colouring and decorative quality make it one of Leicester's finest architectural legacies of the hosiery industry. Its designer, S.H. Langley, was not the best known of Leicester architects of the period, but for Harrison & Hayes he created a building of real quality and originality. Built in 1913 with a single-storey machine shop, it represents a transition from the tall nineteenth cen-

BELOW Former Harrison and Hayes factory, Gateway Street, 1913

LOWER RIGHT Former Luke Turner factory 1893

TOP Terracotta mermaids relief, Royal Doulton Company 1900

ABOVE AND ABOVE RIGHT Former Harrison and Hayes factory: stonework details

FAR RIGHT Former Luke Turner factory

tury factory to the single-storey works which became more common in the 1920s and 1930s. The main material is smooth cream brick and this is set off by details in sandstone and concrete. The composition is completed by a dark green glazed brick base to the ground floor. The side of the building facing Deacon Street is particularly lively: the shallow curved head to the second floor window echoes the curved parapets and inverted arches of the bays of the machine shop.

# 15
# *Making the Town Work*

MANY GEORGIAN TOWNS present a picture of an elegant resort for the leisured classes. Victorian towns, on the other hand, were working communities making goods and producing the wealth which made Britain for a time the richest and most powerful country in the world. The Victorians were fascinated by technology: engineers were extending their science to new limits by building new machines, developing new materials and new ways of using materials, and designing new types of building and methods of construction. Georgian towns are marked by calm Classical repose; Victorian towns offer a bustling mixture of building types and styles.

TOP Beam engine at Abbey Pumping Station, 1891

RIGHT Gas holder, Aylestone Meadows, 1930

The Victorians thought out ways to make their fast growing towns and cities work and to make living in them tolerable. They developed services for the people: schools, libraries, cemeteries, transport, water supply, gas and electricity, and, most important of all, sewers and sewage treatment. To run these services they devised an increasingly democratic machinery for local administration.

There was a debate, just as there is today, about whether services should be provided by the local authority or by private enterprise. In Leicester the Town Council began to build sewers from the middle of the nineteenth century onwards. It is worth reflecting that until then a hole in the ground was the main means of disposing of sewage. In the elegant Georgian residences of the previous century the nightmen would have called each night to collect the day's waste. The biggest advance came in 1885 when the Borough bought land at Beaumont Leys to treat sewage by making it into fertiliser. The system of pipes and pumping station to get the sewage to Beaumont Leys was designed by the Borough Surveyor, Joseph

TOP Gas workers' cottages, Aylestone Road, 1879

RIGHT Gas Service Centre, designed by Architects' Design Group, 1974-76

FAR RIGHT Gas Museum, Aylestone Road

Gordon. Stockdale Harrison designed the building in Corporation Road and the engineers of Gimson and Co. built the four huge beam engines. It is hard for us to see why the pumping of sewage should warrant such a grand building with such highly decorated machinery. But to people who knew what conditions were like in the Victorian town, and whose parents could have remembered epidemics causing hundreds of deaths, the hygienic disposal of sewage was an exciting and noble task.

Gas was another important utility, and it also left its mark on the character of Leicester today. The gas company was formed as early as 1821 and became highly profitable, supplying gas for factories, homes, and street lighting. In 1877 the Council bought the company and in the following year built the new gas works on Aylestone Road. Once again, the buildings reflect the pride and excitement in making the town work. A tall clock tower was built with a row of very distinctive houses for gas workers designed by architects Shenton and Baker in 1879. The houses look quite different from more normal terraced housing of the time with big gables and small-paned windows.

Some of the greatest Victorian monuments were built by the railway companies and railway construction

ABOVE London Road Station facade, 1892

RIGHT Terracotta decoration on London Road railway bridge: the initials and arms of the Midland Railway Company. The bridge was the subject of one of Harry Peach's campaigns against unsightly advertising (see Chapter 26)

had a huge effect in shaping Victorian towns. Leicester's earliest railway was built by Robert Stephenson and had its terminal at the Rally near West Bridge. It was built in 1834 and needed a narrow tunnel nearly a mile long to take it under Glenfield Hill.

The Midland Railway was for many years, until the opening of the Great Central Railway in 1899, the only company connecting Leicester with other major towns. Its London terminal at St Pancras is perhaps the building which, more than any other, sums up the Victorian age and its fascination with technology and travel. The Midland Railway Company built two fine station buildings in Leicester. The original one was a handsome Classical building in Campbell Street. It was from there that the first Cook's Tour left for Loughborough, an event now commemorated by a Statue of Thomas Cook by James Butler at the corner of Station Street and London Road. Only a pair of gatepiers on Station Street remain as evidence of that building as the Company built an entirely new station on London Road in 1892 demolishing the Campbell Street building in the process.

The big arches of the present station frontage with their fine brickwork and *faience* (glazed terracotta) lettering announcing *Departure* and *Arrival* make little sense now that road building has changed the traffic flow in the Station forecourt. But what a sense of anticipation the Victorian traveller must have felt passing under those arches to catch a steam-hauled express to London, Sheffield, or Glasgow. What buildings we might have had if the Victorians had built airports!

TOP Faience *IN* and *OUT* and *DEPARTURE* panels and *ARRIVAL* arch, London Road Station

BELOW RIGHT London Road Station tower

BELOW FAR RIGHT Statue of Thomas Cook by James Butler 1993, with Fred Hamer and Scruff

BELOW Telephone boxes outside London Road Station: made in cast iron to a classic design of 1935 by Giles Gilbert Scott, the architect of Liverpool Anglican Cathedral and Waterloo Bridge in London. Only a handful of boxes of this type survive as listed buildings after their replacement by British Telecom in the 1980s

# 16
# *Death*

THE RAPID GROWTH in the populations of towns and cities in the nineteenth century caused a severe strain on facilities intended to serve much smaller numbers of people. There was a particularly acute problem with the burial of the dead: churchyards became seriously overcrowded and were thought to be sources of disease. A means had to be found that would provide for decent and hygienic burial. Cemeteries developed as a solution to this problem, but they were intended to serve more than just practical purposes. The nineteenth century cemetery was seen as a place where people could stroll for relaxation and where the bereaved could find comfort. The memorials and the picturesque landscape in which they were set were seen as sources of improving thoughts for the visitor.

Leicester's first great cemetery was laid out at Welford Road to the design of Hamilton and Medland in 1849. The layout and planting reflected the ideas of the eminent landscape architect John Claudius Loudon. The Cemetery had separate areas set aside for Anglicans and Nonconformists and originally had Gothic chapels and lodges.

Only the lodge on University Road remains. After suggestions from the City Planning Department

prompted by a local historian, it was rescued from decay by Leicester University and restored and extended to a design by Douglas Smith Stimson Partnership in 1990. The lodge took on a new life as *the Gatehouse*: the University's Chaplaincy Centre.

Welford Road Cemetery makes an important contribution to the quality of Leicester in various ways. It is a collection of memorial sculpture in a wide range of styles: Gothic, Classical, Art Nouveau (see Chapter 18), even Celtic and Moorish. It is a wonderfully romantic piece of landscape with many fine mature trees. The romantic effect is enhanced by the ivy covering many of the memorials although plant growth ultimately damages the stonework.

The Cemetery is also a historical record of Victorian and early twentieth century Leicester. Many of the people mentioned elsewhere in this book are buried there. To take just two examples: Isaac Barradale, architect of some of Leicester's most distinctive late-Victorian buildings, is buried close to University Road; and the Art Nouveau memorial to Arthur Wakerley, who died in 1931, stands on the main avenue from Welford Road. (Wakerley's work will be described in Chapter 26.) The memorials in the Cemetery also bear the names of many of the people who built Leicester's industrial and commercial wealth including, most famously, Thomas Cook (see Chapter 15).

ABOVE From the city of the dead to the living city

FACING PAGE
FAR LEFT Art Nouveau angel on Wakerley family monument (Arthur Wakerley d1931)

FACING PAGE
LEFT *The Gatehouse*: former cemetery lodge extended and converted to a chaplaincy for Leicester University, 1990

BELOW LEFT TO RIGHT
*Time's winged chariot...*

The grave of Thomas Cook d1892

Moorish monument to Charles Wheatley d1886

ABOVE Avenue alongside University Road

RIGHT *Et in Arcadia ego*: Greek monuments to members of the Harris family

# 17
# *Growth and Renewal*

MILL HILL LANE gives a clue to the origins of South Highfields as an area of open farm land to the south of the town. Susanna Watts suggested that visitors climb the steps of one of the mills at the top of London Road hill to get a better view of Charnwood Forest. A map of 1828 shows *Whetstones Mill* roughly on the present site of Mill Hill Lane. The Lane is still narrow and winding in contrast with the grid pattern of the later streets.

Housing grew in this area from the 1830s throughout the rest of the nineteenth century. South Highfields became a prosperous suburb close to the

ABOVE LEFT Teardrop window by Arthur Wakerley, London Road, 1888

ABOVE RIGHT Leicestershire School of Music, College Street, 1836

RIGHT London Road with 7th Day Adventist Church, 1867

TOP CENTRE South Highfields looking east from City Centre

TOP FAR LEFT London Road/University Road, 1867

LOWER FAR LEFT Hobart Street

ABOVE LEFT Tichborne Street, 1877

ABOVE RIGHT Tichborne Street

FACING PAGE BELOW LEFT TO RIGHT

Severn Street

Brookhouse Avenue

Severn Street, 1870s

Synagogue, Highfield Street, 1898

TOP RIGHT Prebend Street, pre-1840

CENTRE RIGHT Marquis Wellington pub, London Road, 1907

ABOVE Upper Tichborne Street, 1880s

TOP RIGHT Prebend Street Gardens, opened 1987

LOWER RIGHT Severn Street: a good omen for the tomato crop

Victorian town and contained a mixture of housing from impressive terraced and detached villas to intimate little streets fitted onto small plots by enterprising developers.

The Collegiate School was designed by the Sheffield architect John Grey Weightman and built in 1836. Its Gothic style reflects its origins as an Anglican school and contrasts with the Classical severity of the Nonconformist Proprietary School (now New Walk Museum). St Peter's Church of 1878 was the work of the eminent architect G.E. Street. The Synagogue, built in 1898, was an example of the taste for the exotic of the architect Arthur Wakerley. Both the Church and the Synagogue were wealthy institutions supported by the prosperous business and professional people living nearby.

The housing grew in patches but followed a general pattern of developing up the hill from Conduit Street towards Evington Road. Despite the use of the familiar red brick and slate, the area has great variety of layout, house size, and above all, of detail. The houses are given individuality by craftsmanship and design and by sometimes highly picturesque doorways, windows, eaves and stone-and plasterwork. In places standardised decoration is used, like the terracotta plant motifs in the eaves of houses in College Avenue. Groups of houses are given nameplates and datestones, like *Coningsby Villas* and *Venetia Villas* of 1883 in Severn Street. It is important that this richness and variety of detail is kept if South Highfields is to continue to make its particular contribution to the quality of Leicester.

The area was prosperous at the beginning of the twentieth century but by the 1960s the type of people who had earlier chosen to live there preferred the suburbs or a home out of the City altogether. The resulting problems of lack of maintenance and poor morale were made worse by a road proposal

RIGHT College Street, probably 1870s

CENTRE RIGHT College Avenue, 1886

BELOW LEFT London Road, Top Hat Terrace, 1864

BELOW RIGHT Brookhouse Avenue, 1888

which affected the area, discouraging investment until it was abandoned in 1973.

But the early 1970s were a time of radical change in thinking on the future of older housing. A decade or two earlier the terraced housing in South Highfields might have been swept away and replaced by completely new development. Instead a Housing Renewal Strategy was drawn up in 1975 by the City Council's planners and it has been implemented in the years since then. The Strategy identified the ninth largest stock of pre-1919 houses and the sixth largest stock of sub-standard houses in the country. It covered 35,000 properties, one third of the housing stock of the City. The implementation of the Strategy forged ways of joint working by the Council and residents and had an effect on the City as profound as many of the historic events described in other pages. South Highfields is a good example, but only one example, of a dramatic and far-reaching movement.

The Renewal Strategy work in South Highfields took place throughout the 1980s. The special architectural character of the area was recognised at the outset by the designation of a conservation area and the introduction of special planning powers to protect the detailed design of individual houses which is so important to safeguarding the overall character of the area. Conserving and renewing the houses went hand in hand and renewal work protected the architectural quality of an area which contains some of the finest nineteenth century housing in the City.

The Strategy worked through grants to owners to encourage them to bring their houses up to modern standards and through powers to acquire properties where the landlord was unwilling to carry out necessary work. Housing associations had a vital role to play in this, and so did the initiative of the residents themselves. Building up the image of the area and its pleasantness as a place to live was also important. Schemes like the gardens in Prebend Street, on the

RIGHT Prebend Street Gardens

FAR RIGHT Severn Street, probably 1870s

CENTRE RIGHT Severn Street, 1883

BOTTOM LEFT Lincoln Street

BOTTOM RIGHT Brookhouse Avenue, gnome sweet gnome

site of some old garages, and the community workshops in a former coach house in Gotham Street, are important examples of improvements aimed to strengthen the environmental quality and social life of the area. Boundary walls are extremely vulnerable to the weather and expensive to rebuild and the area benefited from extensive rebuilding of front and back walls under the Strategy.

Attention has also been given to the important issues of traffic and parking. In the early 1990s the City and County Councils began an ambitious scheme to calm traffic in the Highfields area. The public reaction was favourable and the Highfields scheme has been the forerunner of many more in Leicester and other towns throughout the country.

Priorities under the renewal programme moved on to other areas but the future of South Highfields was not forgotten. Advice is available to property owners on maintenance and security and area caretakers give practical help where it is needed. South Highfields is a story of hard work by residents and the Council to achieve a lasting improvement, and to safeguard the area's special character.

# 18
# *Commerce*

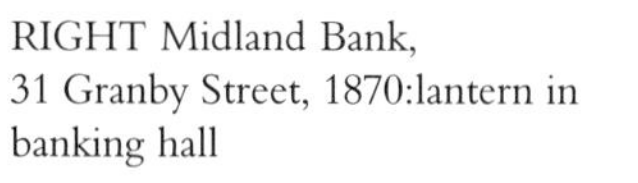

RIGHT Midland Bank, 31 Granby Street, 1870:lantern in banking hall

BELOW RIGHT National Westminster Bank, St Martin's, 1901: the style of the window (on the Hotel Street elevation) is Baroque but the flowing lines of the female figures supporting it are surely a product of the Art Nouveau style which is echoed in ironwork elsewhere on the building.

BELOW LEFT Midland Bank, Granby Street, glazing with flowing lines which seem to anticipate the Art Nouveau style

INDUSTRIAL PROSPERITY brought with it a growth in what is now called the service sector. In Granby Street, banks and other businesses, serving the wealthy industrialists and professional people of the growing town, set up in competition with one another.

In 1869 the architect William Millican designed a building for the National Provincial Bank (now NatWest) at the corner of Granby Street and Horsefair Street. It looks like a *palazzo* or townhouse for a wealthy merchant in Florence or Rome, or like one of the London gentlemen's clubs which were copying Italian styles at the time the bank was built. Millican chose a cool buff brick and stone to give his building an air of sober respectability.

Nearby, at about the same time, Joseph Goddard was designing a headquarters for the Leicestershire Bank (now the Midland Bank). At first he put forward a design quite like Millican's. But the appearance of a bank building was part of its appeal to customers and an Italian palazzo design for the Leicestershire Bank was replaced with something which contrasted with its rival. The result was one of Leicester's most extraordinary buildings. Goddard changed his original Italianate design to one partly in a Gothic style with tall pointed windows. There are influences from northern Italy in the striped arches and in the shape of some of the smaller window openings. The main feature at the corner of Bishop Street is a turret with a *French pavilion* roof. The interior of the banking hall is church-like. The coloured glass has flowing patterns which seem to anticipate the style known as Art Nouveau which was popular on the Continent at the turn of the century. The building is in a mixture of brick, stone and terracotta and was

LEFT TO RIGHT Granby Street, (Belvoir Street), General News Room 1898, Lloyds Bank 1930s, (buildings omitted), Bishop Street, Midland Bank 1872, development on site of former Picture House 1980, 5 Granby Street mid-19th century, National Westminster Bank 1870, (Horsefair Street)

covered with carvings by Samuel Barfield, the sculptor who made the statues for the Clock Tower.

Joseph Goddard and his partners, including his son Henry Langton Goddard, made a very big impression on Victorian Leicester, designing many fine and important buildings in a variety of architectural styles. In 1898 they designed the General News Room, later the Yorkshire Bank, at the corner of Granby Street and Belvoir Street. The Baroque style came originally from Italy in the sixteenth century. It was used in many countries in Europe and there are local variations. In Britain Baroque was popular at the end of the seventeenth century and early in the eighteenth, but it was revived at the end of the nineteenth century and used especially for large public and commercial buildings. The General News Room is typical, using columns and other elements of Classical architecture but exaggerating scales and introducing sculpture to give an effect of swirling movement rather than the calm, still appearance of a Classical building like 17 Friar Lane.

Away from Granby Street, in St Martin's, is another fine Baroque commercial building. The National Westminster Bank (built for Pares' Bank and later taken over by Parr's Bank) was built to the design of S. Perkin Pick in 1900. Overall the building is calmer in mood than the General News Room but has a lively skyline with domes and tall chimney stacks. Flowing lines are introduced in delightful sculpted relief panels on the front of the building and in the Art Nouveau ironwork.

The Grand Hotel, designed by Cecil Ogden with Simpson and Harvey in 1896, adds further to the varied pattern of styles in Granby Street. The architects mixed styles freely in an eclectic approach typical of the late Victorian period when earlier rigid attitudes to architecture were breaking down. The hotel has echoes of French and German architecture of the sixteenth century. For the corner tower the architects returned to home, apparently basing their design on the churches of Sir Christopher Wren. Add

just a hint of Dutch in the gables and the building has a skyline worthy of Disneyland. Corner buildings make a particularly important contribution to the street scene and the Grand builds up from the first floor, with three levels of columns supported by great stone brackets and topped by the tower, to make a powerful corner feature.

The mixture of styles does not stop with the Grand Hotel. At the corner of Chatham Street is a building with a Flemish stepped gable and there is delicate decorative ironwork at number 80.

The Turkey Cafe, designed by Arthur Wakerley in 1901, uses colourful glazed terracotta by William Neatby of the Doulton Company. It shows Wakerley's interest in exotic and extravagant designs. He was clearly aware of the Art Nouveau movement which made a great impact at the end of the nineteenth century in countries like France and Belgium but was limited in its influence in England. Art Nouveau broke away from historical styles of architecture and decoration and was characterised by the use of flowing and sinuous curved lines often based on plants, hair, or the human form.

Much plainer than all these showpieces on the main thoroughfare is the row of factories in York Street. They are impressive in a different way, looking more typical of a Lancashire cotton town than the more mixed and small-scale streets of Leicester.

The inter-war period brought some further contributions to Granby Street. A castle-like Victorian Post Office was knocked down to make way for a plain 1930s commercial building at the corner of Bishop Street. Next to it is a much more delicate thirties building, Lloyds Bank. At the entrance to Granby Street near the station, the building now occupied by Blunts' Shoes was designed by Symington Prince and

Pike in the 1930s. It uses a mixture of white Portland stone, green Spanish tiles, and bronze to make a highly individual gatepost to the street.

Recent decades have had a mixed effect on Granby Street. What was once the main road from Leicester to London has now been made into a quiet shopping street by measures to control through traffic. At the southern end the inner ring road forms a barrier between the City Centre and the station and pedestrians are directed through a subway. The link with the railway station, which should be one of the most important focal points of a city centre, is disrupted and the visitor arriving by train is faced with tarmac and traffic where the opportunity once existed to create a public square and bus interchange.

FACING PAGE TOP LEFT National Westminster Bank, St Martin's

FACING PAGE TOP RIGHT Turkey Cafe, 24 Granby Street, 1901

FACING PAGE BOTTOM LEFT Grand Hotel, 1896 and later

RIGHT Factories in York Street, late 19th century

FAR RIGHT The City Gallery, 90 Granby Street, Richard Perry exhibition 1995

BELOW LEFT Turkey Cafe, 24 Granby Street, one of the turkeys made for the 1983 restoration by Hathernware Ceramics

BELOW RIGHT Blunts' Shoes (formerly Harris's of Granby Corner), 128-132 Granby Street, 1930s

The Town Hall, 1876: the Queen Anne design was chosen in competition against Classical and Gothic entries.

# 19
# *Civic Pride*

TOWN HALL SQUARE today is a space of quiet civic dignity, but until 1866 it was the cattle market and the traders and others who made their living there had resisted all attempts to move them. With its pubs, bustle, noise and smells, it made a very different contribution then to Leicester's character.

Bishop Street Methodist Church, dated 1815, is a witness to the period before the Town Hall changed this part of Leicester. It is Classical and simple: the design of the front elevation echoes Friars' Mills or 17 Friar Lane, buildings intended for entirely different purposes. It is in the Leicester tradition of red brick with a little stonework, harmonising with the later buildings.

During the second half of the nineteenth century towns outside London were anxious to establish their own distinct identity. This local pride, mixed with social concern, led to the foundation of schools and hospitals, museums and art galleries. The corporations of Victorian towns vied with each other also in building magnificent town halls for their meetings and civic gatherings, as offices and sometimes as concert halls and courts. Many of these Victorian town halls are grandiose and in the prevailing styles of the day: Classical magnificence at Leeds, Gothic grandeur at Manchester.

Leicester departed from this trend. The Council chose what, for the early 1870s, was a very modern and unusual design by a young local architect, Francis Hames, whose only earlier work in the town was a group of shops in Silver Street. Hames was working in the office of a much better known London architect, W.E. Nesfield, and the Town Hall appears to be heavily influenced by Nesfield's work. The style used

RIGHT The Town Hall: civic buildings of a later generation loom behind

BELOW Facade to the Sun Alliance Building (now Trustee Savings Bank), 1891

for the Town Hall is based loosely on English building at the time of Queen Anne in the early eighteenth century. The warm red brick and cream stone, with details like the panels on the ground floor frontage showing a duck welcoming the dawn and an owl representing night, make the Town Hall a friendly, even a quirky, building. Sunflowers were a favourite motif of the Queen Anne movement and occur on the Town Hall and several other buildings of the period in Leicester.

If architectural styles can reflect the attitudes of the people the buildings are designed for, Leicester's Town Hall gives a more open and approachable impression of the Victorian local authority than the monumental civic palaces in other cities. In some ways the Town Hall typifies qualities of the City described elsewhere in this book: expressing the pride of the borough modestly rather than by pomposity or ostentation.

The new Town Hall needed a suitable setting and Hames designed a square to set it off soon after the Town Hall itself was built. As a feature to catch the eye, Sir Israel Hart donated the bronze fountain in 1879. Again Hames did the design with Ionic columns

ABOVE Town Hall Square: redesigned and laid out 1987-89

RIGHT The Leicester Maze, 1992

and winged lions. Oporto in Portugal has an identical fountain, apparently cast in Paris from the Leicester pattern.

It was not long before other fine buildings were attracted to the square and by the early twentieth century the buildings around it had taken on something like their present appearance. On the north side the Goddard firm of architects designed a red brick building in a mixed, largely Flemish, style in 1891. It was the subject of a planning battle in the early 1970s when it was proposed to pull the building down and redevelop the site. After the City Council had op-

Rear elevation of the Picture House, 1924, now incorporated into an office and shopping development

posed the demolition, the Secretary of State for the Environment gave permission for the scheme to go ahead with the retention of the facade to Horsefair Street.

In the first few years of the twentieth century Town Hall Square was chosen as the site for Leicester's memorial to the dead of the South African War. The monument, a granite wall with bronze angels in flowing robes, was made by the sculptor Crosland McLure.

On the east side of the square is a contrasting building which sets off the prevailing pattern of red brick and buff or creamy stone. The back of what was one of Leicester's early cinemas is in white Portland stone from Dorset with a huge three-part window. It is a showy building appropriate for its original use as a cinema and adds a touch of panache to an otherwise calm and ordered scene.

In 1987 the City and County Councils drew up a set of ideas for improving the City Centre. A new layout for Town Hall Square came high on their list and the present design with paths radiating from the fountain was carried out and opened in 1989. Its best features were the opening-up of a new space for pedestrians in front of the Town Hall - previously this was a car park - and the restoration of railings guarded by cast iron lions. Francis Hames would surely approve of the setting of his building today: a space which would grace any city in Britain.

# 20
# *Breathing Space*

UNTIL THE 1870s Leicester had developed as a maze of streets full of terraced houses and factories but with little open space where the people of the town could relax during their scarce leisure time. Today, parks and open spaces are as important to the City as buildings and streets. But all the City's parks, except New Walk and Nelson Mandela Park (laid out as Welford Road Recreation Ground), have been provided since 1880.

In other cities, local benefactors came forward to finance public parks but in Leicester the Town Council decided to take the initiative itself. The opportunity came in 1878 when a plan was drawn up to relieve flooding from the River Soar near the Abbey site. Doubts were cast on the wisdom of making the land into a park because of the frequent flooding, but the Council went ahead with a design competition which was won by Barron and Sons of Derby.

The original design with winding walks, a lake, and generous tree cover, still dictates the shape of the Park today. Sports grounds included bowling greens, tennis and croquet courts and an archery ground. There were greenhouses and an American Garden. The layout had an overall feel of natural countryside but it included formal gardens. The Prince and Princess of Wales opened

RIGHT Abbey Park: the Lake and Chinese Friendship Garden

ABOVE Abbey Park Bridge, c1930

TOP RIGHT Ruins of Cavendish House, c1600

RIGHT AND FAR RIGHT Abbot Penny's Wall, c1500: initials JPC may stand for *John Penny construxit.*

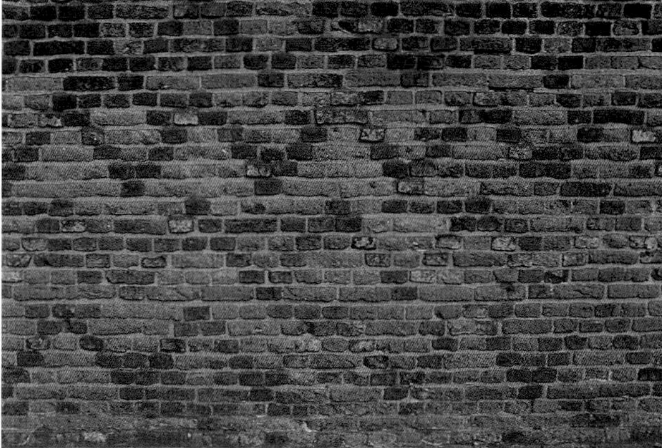

the Park amid scenes of great civic splendour on 29th May 1882. Train excursions were run to bring visitors from other cities to see the opening events.

The next important development in the history of the Park came in 1925 when the Abbey Grounds were incorporated into it. This part of Abbey Park has a distinct 1930s atmosphere with a cafe, shelters and gatepiers, all in the style of the time.

The Abbey itself was one of the largest houses of the Augustinian Order in England. It was founded in about 1138 and had an important role in the mediaeval town. The layout marked out in low walls on the lawns may show the basic shape of the mediaeval Abbey.

Close to Abbey Park Road are the remains of what was once one of the most magnificent houses in Leicester. Cavendish House was the home of the Countess of Devon. It was built in about 1600 but had a short life, being burnt down in the Civil War in 1645. It has survived as a gaunt and romantic ruin.

But the most fascinating feature of the Abbey Grounds is the wall around them, especially the brick section running along Abbey Lane. After Britain ceased to be part of the Roman Empire the art of making and laying bricks was lost. It started to appear again in Leicestershire at about the end of the fifteenth century. Kirby Muxloe Castle was built about twenty years before Abbot Penny's Wall. There the bricks were made on the site but the work was supervised by a man from Belgium and the masons were sent to Tattershall Castle in Lincolnshire to learn about making and laying bricks. The abbot at Leicester at the end of the fifteenth century was John Penny and the wall includes his initials formed in blue bricks dating it to around 1500, some of the earliest post-Roman brickwork in England. It is worth carefully crossing Abbey Lane to see the brick patterns from the other side of the road as the wall is one of the most interesting structures in Leicester.

Open spaces, trees, and gardens express the purpose of the Park but buildings are also important. The spire of St Mark's Church is a reminder that the Park was right next to one of the poorest parts of the Victorian town which St Mark's was built to serve.

Inside the Park, lodges, a bandstand and shelters all provide landmarks. Today Abbey Park is much used by Leicester's Asian community and the multi-cultural atmosphere, as well as Leicester's twinning links with the Chinese city of Chongqing, is reflected in the Chinese Friendship Garden. Its bridge and pagoda were made in the Belgrave Community Workshops in 1987. They would not have looked out of place in the Park of 1882 and are reminiscent of exotic garden buildings in Victorian gardens like Biddulph Grange in Staffordshire. Ideas for the future development of the Park in the twenty-first century include gardens and other projects that express the City's cultural diversity.

The Victorian founders of the Park may have enjoyed some of the intriguing works of art now placed there. One of these, Steve Geliot's *Islands and Insulators* from 1989, sets a frame for views of the Park beside the artist's mysterious carved images. The Redland Garden of the Senses combines sculpture with plants specially chosen to stimulate the senses of touch, smell, hearing and sight.

RIGHT *Islands and Insulators* by Steve Geliot, 1989

FAR RIGHT Gate lodge, James Tait, 1882

BELOW LEFT TO RIGHT

Plaque marking opening of Abbey Park

The Redland Garden of the Senses, 1995

Ironwork and stonework on gates to Abbey Park Road

*Islands and Insulators* detail

FACING PAGE

TOP Abbey Park: bandstand and spire of St Mark's Church

BOTTOM Bridge forming part of the Chinese Friendship Garden, 1987

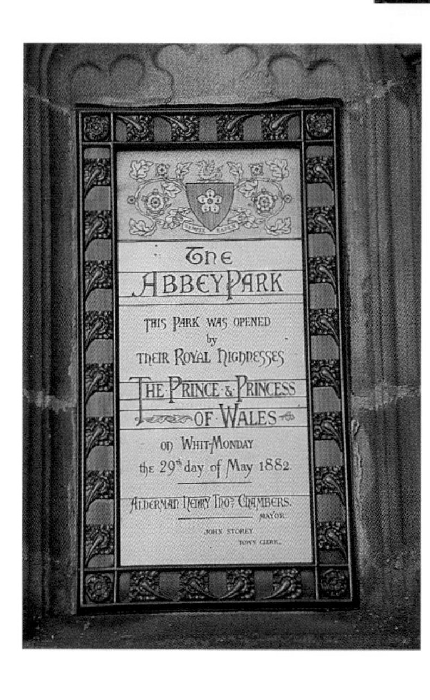

# 21
# *Goddard and Barradale*

THE SUBURBS of the early nineteenth century are now part of the inner city. As the century went on Leicester expanded into areas which are within walking distance of the City Centre and which we

FACING PAGE Church of St John the Baptist 1885, baptistery

ABOVE 2 Springfield Road, c1850

TOP RIGHT
4 and 6 Springfield Road, 1894

MIDDLE RIGHT
31 Springfield Road, 1890s, moulded brickwork

BOTTOM RIGHT
25 Springfield Road, 1982-83

now think of as fairly central. Springfield Road and the parallel part of Clarendon Park Road contain many of the elements of Stoneygate, the prosperous southern suburb of the Victorian town.

The story starts at 2 Springfield Road. When it was built in 1850 the Classical house, now behind lawns and cedar trees, was set in open country with just a few substantial houses. Next door is a complete contrast. 4 and 6 Springfield Road were designed by the Goddard practice in 1894 in a style by then becoming a little unfashionable. The houses were similar to some of the work of the architect Norman Shaw who led a move away from ornate mid-Victorian architectural styles to design simpler buildings based on historic English architecture. 4 and 6 Springfield Road have big gables, windows with small panes, and a timber balcony with turned balusters running along the frontage.

25 Springfield Road contrasts with the older terraces and detached houses nearby. Its architect was Theo Matoff, then head of the School of Architecture at Leicester Polytechnic, and it was built in 1982-3. The plain red brick cube is disciplined and uncompromisingly modern but echoes the houses around it in its pattern of windows and roof slopes.

On the London Road frontage, between Springfield Road and Clarendon Park Road is Clarendon Park Congregational Church, designed by James Tait and built in 1885-86 in granite from Mountsorrel. It has a

ABOVE Church of St John the Baptist, nave and chancel

broad west tower and unusual tracery in some of the windows, particularly the zigzag pattern of the windows facing Springfield Road.

We have seen some of the buildings of the Goddard practice who did much to form the character of Victorian Leicester. Particular local architects could stamp their personality on a town: in Princess Road East, for example, Joseph Goddard designed all the houses on the south side between West Walk and University Road.

The Church of St John the Baptist in Clarendon Park Road is one of Goddard's masterpieces. It was built in 1885 under the patronage of Miss Sarah Barlow. Outside, the church is quite plain but impressive in scale and detail with sheer brick walls and a big tiled roof. A little spire or *fleche* gives it a vertical note and ventilates the roofspace. The interior is a marvel: those high walls and the big roof are supported by internal buttresses which form tunnel-like aisles and a gallery. At the west end is a dark and mysterious baptistery. These secret spaces contrast dramatically with the light and airy nave and chancel.

FACING PAGE RIGHT
Church of St John the Baptist, Clarendon Park Road, note the small lead-covered spire or *fleche* and the *plate tracery* (openings cut out of a slab of stone) in the windows.

RIGHT Clarendon Park Congregational Church, London Road, 1885-86

BELOW LEFT UPPER
7 St John's Road, built for woodcarver Thomas Birch, who made the porch and front door, and named after his wife Amelia Fleetwood, 1890.

BELOW LEFT LOWER
Houses with Flemish gables, 15-17 St John's Road, c1890

BELOW RIGHT 6 Clarendon Park Road, 1884

Another of the architects who most helped to give Leicester its character was Isaac Barradale. Next to the church are two pairs of semi-detached houses designed by Barradale which typify Stoneygate and larger houses built in Leicester in the 1880s and 1890s. Similar designs were used in Stoneygate Road and Knighton Road. Many other Leicester houses of the period echo the pattern of huge projecting gables, big brick chimneys and plenty of decorative woodwork, sometimes elaborately turned or carved. In the 1890s Barradale designed three fine houses in St John's Road: number 7 is Dutch in style and there is a Flemish pair, much like town houses in Bruges, at 15 and 17.

Inglewood, 1892

# 22
# *Arts and Crafts*

ALTHOUGH, as the previous chapter shows, there are a few earlier houses, Stoneygate really grew from the 1870s onwards. It was favoured by the industrialists and professional people who were becoming prosperous in the Victorian town. Many of the houses in Stoneygate were built in the form of miniature country estates with lodges, stables, large gardens, and sweeping drives leading to the front door. The development of Stoneygate continues today. Those large houses, designed to have a staff of servants, grooms, and gardeners, do not suit the lifestyle of people in modern Leicester. They tend to become divided into flats or used as care homes or student houses. Not everyone can maintain a big garden without help and there is pressure to subdivide plots to build separate new houses. So the character of the area changes over the years, but Stoneygate remains a very distinctive area of Leicester, with grand houses, and spacious, tree-lined streets.

Knighton Spinneys marks Joseph Goddard's advancing career as an architect and businessman. In 1875 he had designed a house for himself in University Road. 1885 found him moving 'up-market' to a full scale town mansion in Ratcliffe Road with a set of outbuildings. Goddard had a fashionable interest in the architecture of English manor houses and cottages and this is shown in his design. He called for a range of craftsman's skills from his builders with timber, brickwork, wood carving, tiles and leadwork.

The architect Stockdale Harrison also drew from historical English architecture in his work at the turn of the century. His house at 15 Elms Road, built in 1894, reflects this interest with timber work in the big overhanging gables and Classical touches in the doorway

ABOVE Knighton Spinneys, 1885

ABOVE RIGHT 15 Elms Road, 1894

RIGHT Inglewood from the garden: the big curved bay was an addition.

and plaster work. At 147 Ratcliffe Road the influence is from the early eighteenth century expressed in fine brickwork, regularly spaced brackets *(modillions)* at the eaves, and dormer windows with shallow curved heads.

At the junction of Ratcliffe Road and Elms Road is Inglewood, a house designed for his own use by one of the most famous figures in Victorian Leicester. Ernest Gimson was born in Leicester in 1864. His father was an industrialist who owned a heavy engineering company. Ernest trained as an architect in Leicester, with Isaac Barradale, and in London. He became one of the leading figures in the Arts and Crafts movement which aimed to renew interest in traditional craftsmanship as a response to growing mass production. He also trained as a furniture maker and in plaster work, believing that a designer should also be able to master practical skills. The Leicester area has a number of Ernest Gimson's works as an architect and there is a collection of his furniture in Newarke Houses Museum. Gimson furniture is ranked among the finest products of British craftsmanship and can also be seen in collections in Cheltenham and in museums around the world. In 1892 Gimson began to base his life in the Cotswolds

RIGHT Inglewood

LOWER RIGHT Inglewood, decorative plasterwork, 1892

eventually settling at Sapperton in Gloucestershire where he died in 1919.

Inglewood, built in 1892, shows Gimson's concerns quite clearly. Although it is a large house, the design is simple and there is little decoration. Instead, the quality of the house depends on carefully worked out proportions and beautiful materials: local brick and Swithland slate. A particular feature is the *catslide* roof on the right hand side of the frontage sweeping down from the ridge to form a porch over the front door. The slates range from tiny ones at the top to large flags at the eaves. The beautifully kept garden was also first laid out by Gimson and makes a perfect setting for the house.

Leicester would be lucky if Ernest Gimson had designed only Inglewood in the City. But in 1898 he

built another house, this time for his brother Arthur. The White House, on North Avenue, is also based on English cottage architecture. Like Inglewood it is a fairly large house but differs from other big Stoneygate houses in the simplicity of its design. Again its beauty lies in the materials-limewashed brick and

TOP The White House, 1898, garden elevation: plaster decoration on bays by G.P. Bankart

ABOVE LEFT The White House,

ABOVE RIGHT The White house, detail of gutters and hopper head

Swithland slate - and in its proportions. Details like the curved brackets supporting the gutters look elegant while doing their job efficiently: the essence of fine design. Gimson did indulge in a little decoration although it is not normally visible from the street. Facing the garden there are two bays with decorative plasterwork by G.P. Bankart, another Leicester man and a friend of Gimson, who gained national recognition for his work in reviving and practising traditional craftsmanship in plaster and lead.

Ernest Gimson's belief in the value of practical craftsmanship is shown in his buildings and in his furniture. Ironically, the high standards he strove for made his furniture very expensive, far beyond the pockets of the ordinary people he had originally hoped would buy it. But it was the skills of thousands of designers and craftspeople as well as those who did the heavy work of building and making building materials, which made Victorian Leicester. Gimson recognised this and embodied it in his work: his houses are an architectural asset to Leicester and their quality is recognised far outside the boundaries of the City.

*(Inglewood and the White House are private homes and are not open to the public).*

# 23
# *Terraces*

THE GROWTH OF LEICESTER in the last quarter of the nineteenth century produced hundreds of streets of terraced, red brick, slate-roofed houses. Some observers have condemned these streets as dull and monotonous but this assessment is superficial. When they were built there were still hundreds of families living in unhealthy and overcrowded housing from

ABOVE View across Highfields from Imperial Hotel towards City Centre

FACING PAGE Terraced houses climb the hill on Hartington Road, 1890s

earlier decades. For them the red brick terraces of areas like Highfields must have seemed highly desirable. These terraces are still providing good homes at a time when housing built in more recent, supposedly more enlightened, times has been demolished and replaced. Driving or passing by train through an area of terraced streets may give an impression of uniformity: this is changed on walking along the streets and looking at the details which give individuality to houses and groups of houses. Much of Leicester's terraced housing was built on flat sites. But in places the terraces, with their rows of chimney stacks, swoop down hills giving genuine drama to the street scene. Hartington Road and the streets around it, where the terraces climb the ridge between Melbourne Road and Mere Road, is an example.

Whatever shortcomings it may have had by today's standards, Leicester's housing of the later nineteenth century had a reputation for being healthy and spacious, especially compared with the severe housing problems of some other cities. The local authority tried to control the quality of housing throughout the nineteenth century and this process was given impetus by the great reforms of the 1875 Public Health Act. The bye-laws which followed set out standards for street widths and lengths which tended to produce regular patterns of terraced housing. The Hartington Road and Vulcan Road area developed plot by plot throughout the 1880s and 1890s, although some of the streets were laid out earlier: Frederick Road, for example, in 1877. Together they seem more like a Pennine town in Yorkshire or Lancashire than the generally flatter Leicester.

The area tells a story of the Victorian community who first lived in it. Life revolved around the factory, school, church or chapel, for some the pub, and later the cinema.

The factories are grouped around the bottom of the hill close to Humberstone Road. The most impressive is the Vulcan Works designed in 1876 by J.B.Everard for Josiah Gimson. It was here that the money was made to enable Ernest Gimson, Josiah's son, to devote his life to the gentlemanly pursuits of architecture and furniture design (see Chapter 22).

The school was in Charnwood Street, built in 1875 and one of a number designed by one of the best of

TOP Frederick Road, laid out in 1877 with houses mainly of the 1880s, and St Saviour's Church, 1875-77

ABOVE LEFT Detail of entry gate and lintel, Frederick Road area

ABOVE RIGHT Former Melbourne Road Chapel, now a Hindu centre

Leicester's Victorian architects, Edward Burgess. It was one of the Board Schools, another social reforming venture of the later nineteenth century, proclaiming the new importance of education by its tower and spire.

Many of the major denominations built churches in the area. Despite Leicester's dominance by Nonconformists, the Church of England had the best site for St Saviour's on the ridge top as it descends towards Humberstone Road. The view along Frederick Road is spectacular. St Saviour's is one of the biggest churches in the City and was designed by Sir George Gilbert Scott. Scott was one of the most eminent architects of the Victorian period and his buildings include the Foreign Office and the hotel at St Pancras Station in London. He, or his practice, also designed many churches all over the country including four in Leicester. For St Saviour's, Scott chose an early Gothic style based on English church architecture of around 1200. Inside there is marvellous craftsmanship in brick and stout columns in red Shap granite from Cumbria.

The pub, the Imperial Hotel, was built as a temperance hotel by Arthur Wakerley and originally had a dome on its tower.

Now the area tells a different story. The Asian community has fashioned a new character from the streets around Hartington Road. The local mosque is an important focus for the lives of the Muslim community. The former Melbourne Road chapel has a new life as the Shree Mandhata Samaj Sahayak Mandal, a major Hindu centre.

What was once the Melbourne Cinema, most recently the Apsara, is empty awaiting a new use. Gimson's works has been subdivided into four factory units by the City Council.

RIGHT Charnwood Street School, 1875

LOWER RIGHT Shopfronts installed under the Housing Renewal Strategy, Vulcan Road

The dominance of the school in Charnwood Street remains constant: education is as important for the local community today as it was to their Victorian predecessors.

Vulcan Road was one of the first areas in Leicester to undergo a co-ordinated effort to improve the condition of houses and the environment around them. The Vulcan Road General Improvement Area was designated and administered by the City Council in the early 1970s before new legislation paved the way for the more comprehensive approach taken after the Renewal Strategy of 1975 was launched. Not all the work is obvious to a casual observer but it has probably been a major reason for the health of both the housing in the area and the local community. One visible effect is the introduction of shopfronts on the thriving corner shops which match the Victorian character of the houses around them. Many of the details of the terraced houses have been fully revealed by cleaning, helped by grants from the City Council.

Most of the houses have lost their original windows and many their original doors and roofing material. Not everything can or should be conserved and no building material or component lasts for ever. But the original windows and doors were probably made especially for the house, maybe by a craftsman with a workshop in a neighbouring street. They are often replaced by products made in a large factory and sold through builder's merchant's chains offering identical standardised products all over the country. Every time this happens a small part of the special local character of the street and the City is lost.

RIGHT Alexandra House: terracotta detail with Atlas figure

# 24
# *A Change of Scale*

SO FAR the character of Leicester has been portrayed as mostly small scale and intimate. But Rutland Street and the streets around it are dominated by big buildings. The interest of this part of the City comes from differences in building type and size and in the layout of the streets and open spaces. Wimbledon Street is canyon-like and dominated by the clatter of knitting machines. The Odeon acts as a great hinge, turning the corner in Rutland Street. St George's Churchyard is secluded and shady.

The best building, and it is a magnificent one, is Alexandra House, at the corner of Rutland Street and Southampton Street. It was designed by Edward Burgess as a bootlace warehouse for Faire Bros. in 1897. Burgess chose light brown terracotta to face the building. Terracotta is a durable material made of fine fired clay which can be easily moulded. For Alexandra House Burgess chose to echo the architecture of Ren-

BELOW LEFT TO RIGHT: Alexandra House, 1897; The Odeon, 1938; 37-43 Rutland Street, 1890. (architects Harding and Toppott.) A suitable development in the foreground would bring this collection of buildings together into a unified street scene.

St George's Churchyard: Church built 1823-27, largely rebuilt 1912-13

aissance Italy to produce a highly decorated facade which was crowned by a corner dome until bomb damage during the Second World War. The building is full of delightful details, brought out by a clean-up scheme sponsored by the City Council in 1990. Two which are particularly worth noting are the terracotta figures of men *(Atlantes)* holding up the big brackets below the top floor windows, and the Southampton Street nameplate formed in terracotta to match the rest of the building. At street level there is a plinth of Norwegian *larvikite*, a dark grey, granite-like stone.

At 78-80 Rutland Street is one of the most curious buildings in Leicester. It was a warehouse built in 1923 and designed by the Leicester architects Fosbrooke and Bedingfield. Like many industrial buildings by that time, it was built around a concrete frame rather than having thick walls supporting the weight of the floors and the roof. Some of the decoration is Gothic but the building is very hard to describe in terms of English architectural styles. The explanation may be that it was built for an American firm of leather importers, Pfister and Vogel, and the design might have been based on their headquarters building in Philadelphia.

The type of building which most typifies the 1930s is the cinema. The Odeon fits into the pattern of big, boldly-designed buildings in Rutland Street although it is quite different from its neighbours. The architect was Robert Bullivant who worked in the Birmingham office of Harry Weedon. Weedon's firm designed Odeons up and down the country, now recognised as some of the best buildings of their time. Prompted by Oscar Deutsch, who established the Odeon organisation *(Oscar Deutsch Entertains Our Nation)*, Weedon devised a completely modern style to suit the modern form of entertainment on offer

RIGHT AND BELOW RIGHT
78-80 Rutland Street, 1923

FAR RIGHT TOP Alexandra
House: ceiling of vestibule

LOWER FAR RIGHT
Alexandra House: street
nameplate in terracotta

BELOW LEFT Alexandra
House: plinth of larvikite and
terracotta detail

inside. Faience was a favourite material and was used to great effect on the Leicester Odeon.

The factory at the corner of Colton Street, which adds buff brick and stone to the diverse palette of building materials in Rutland Street, was originally built for Tyler Brothers in 1875. It is in a mixture of Italian styles and its most intriguing features are circular panels on either side of the doorway with figures of Minerva, a Roman goddess, holding a railway engine, and the god Mercury holding a ship. The figures were carved by Samuel Barfield whose work had already appeared at the Midland Bank in Granby Street. Today, industrial buildings tend to be plain and functional but many Victorian industrialists preferred very showy buildings that would act as advertisements for their business, appearing on trade literature and stationery.

A little way down Colton Street is the Guildhall of the Leicestershire Guild of the Disabled. It is another

ABOVE Leicestershire Guild of the Disabled, Colton Street, 1909

FAR RIGHT Factory at corner of Colton Street and Rutland Street, 1875
with RIGHT figures of Minerva and Mercury

very distinctive building from 1909 designed by architects A.E. and T. Sawday. The style is partly Arts and Crafts but might have been influenced by architecture of the time in the United States. It was built for people who spent their time in wheelchairs or who had to lie in spinal carriages and was designed throughout for disabled access, with features like level thresholds and wide doors.

In 1981 the City Council appointed the country's first full-time Access Officer to work in the City Planning Department. Her job was to encourage the improvement and adaptation of public buildings and spaces to enable people with disabilities to make better use of them, and to spread awareness of the design principles involved. The need for this measure of equality is now widely recognised and supported but it is interesting to note that the Colton Street Guildhall was built to be fully used by people with disabilities over eighty years ago.

An area with such a mixed collection of large buildings can absorb new additions fairly easily. The former City Transport depot built by the Corporation in 1966, a modern building faced in light grey tile and with large areas of glass, could look out of place in other streets but here it sits quite comfortably among a collection of highly individual buildings.

RIGHT AND FAR RIGHT Leicestershire Guild of the Disabled: window details

BELOW LEFT Office and housing development, Rutland Street and Yeoman Street, 1990

BELOW RIGHT 76 Rutland Street, arch and decorative ironwork

By 1990 building styles had changed and become much more varied and decorative than they had been in the earlier post-war decades. The building at the corner of Rutland Street and Yeoman Street, which combines offices and flats, reflects this with arched windows and patterns made by red, yellow and brown brick. Its architect, John Noah, designed a building in which the Victorians might have found familiar echoes.

But something is missing from Rutland Street: the site opposite the Odeon is the focal point of the street as it changes direction. A building or feature is needed here which will transform the street from a collection of fine buildings to a distinct place in which the buildings fit together to form a larger street scene. Interesting proposals have been put forward but building on the site will probably have to await more prosperous times in the development industry.

TOP West Bridge, 1890

ABOVE Riverside Park: Aylestone Bowl with boardwalks

# 25
# *Riverside*

LEICESTER is where it is because Iron Age people, and later the Romans, could cross the River Soar here. The number of place names which include the word bridge or ford is evidence of the great historical importance of rivers and crossing places and of the prosperity they could bring to centres of trade and manufacturing. Although not the largest of rivers, the Soar and its parallel system of canals still form one of the main arteries which shape the City and an obstacle to circulation. They have also offered the City the chance to create a new facility for Leicester people and visitors over the past twenty years and to make an enormous improvement in Leicester's environment.

West Bridge, near the site of the original river crossing, has undergone many changes. The older of the two present bridges was designed by Borough Engineer E.C. Mawby in 1890 and built by John Butler and Co. of Leeds. Until the nineteenth century, West Bridge would have been the main entrance to the town and it is still the most important point of entry to the City Centre. The modern concrete bridge was built by Leicestershire County Council in the late 1970s to take the eastbound traffic coming into the City Centre.

Bridges are also important in history and folklore. A plaque on the nearby Bow Bridge, on the old course of the River Soar, records the legend of Richard III who crossed it twice in 1485: the first time as he rode out to the Battle of Bosworth, the second when his body was brought back from the battlefield slung over a horse. The victorious new king, Henry VII might have passed the same way on his entry into Leicester to proclaim the beginning of the Tudor age: events commemorated by a plaque on the boundary wall to Castle House in Castle Street.

RIGHT Bede House Towpath Bridge over Old River Soar 1887, (modified Warren truss with curved flanges) and Upperton Road Bridge 1890

BELOW Bow Bridge, 1862: decorated with the roses of the houses of Lancaster and York and the cinquefoil of Leicester.

The Mile Straight was canalised in 1889-90 as part of a scheme to relieve flooding and three bridges were provided to cross it. Two were built by the Gimson company in 1890 to very similar designs. They appear to express modern design principles in that they show clearly the way in which they were put together and the reason why they stand up. Horizontal girders supporting the road deck are slung between shallow iron arches spanning the water. Decoration was saved for the abutments where the sandstone piers are designed as obelisks at Walnut Street and as Towers of the Winds from ancient Athens on the Mill Lane Bridge.

The Newarke Bridge opened up a previously isolated corner of the City in 1898. Again Mawby was the designer and his elegant bridge is formed from two unreinforced concrete arches clad in stone in a Gothic

RIGHT Aylestone Meadows

BELOW LEFT TO RIGHT

Bow Bridge: plaque recording the legend of Richard III

Walnut Street Bridge: obelisk pier

Mill Lane Bridge with Tower of the Winds pier

Mill Lane Bridge and Russells' factory, 1925

ABOVE Newarke Bridge, 1898

TOP RIGHT Liberty Works, 1919, beside Walnut Street Bridge/Upperton Road Bridge

RIGHT Plaque fixed in 1985 marking 500th anniversary of the Battle of Bosworth, Castle Street

design appropriate for its position close to the Castle. The bridge was opened by Arthur Wakerley in his year of office as Mayor.

Further south, at Aylestone, there is a group of structures which trace much of the history of bridge building in the City. The bridge which carries the Great Central Way over the River is simple and structurally explicit with braced ironwork supporting the deck between massive abutments in Staffordshire blue brick. It was built for the Great Central Railway Company, opened in 1899, to carry express trains to London, Manchester, and the West Country.

Over a number of years, starting in the late 1970s, the redundant track bed was converted by the City Council to a recreational route for cyclists, walkers and horse riders.

A simple brick arch carries Marsden Lane over the River close to King's Lock. The lock has its own red brick bridge. Nearby is the fifteenth-century Packhorse Bridge which provided a route for horses carrying coal from Swannington. The bridge stretches over the water and marshy meadowland in a series of

TOP Great Central Railway Bridge, Aylestone, c1899

ABOVE Marsden Lane Bridge, Aylestone, probably late 18th century

low stone arches. The River Soar and its tributaries would once have flowed through a wide marshy valley and the mediaeval West Bridge might well have looked like the Packhorse Bridge. The watercourses have been changed to help navigation and to prevent flooding and the valley now forms the Riverside Park.

The Riverside Park ranks with the Housing Renewal Strategy as one of the most far-reaching improvements to Leicester's environment in recent decades. In the early 1970s the Riverside was an untidy and even dangerous part of the City, largely derelict and rarely visited for legitimate purposes. Today it is an eight-mile long public park forming a green ribbon through the City from Watermead Park in the north to Blue Bank Lock in the south. Its 985 hectares include grazing land, formal parks, sports pitches, woods, lakes and marshland. The Park caters for a wide variety of recreational activities from canoeing to bird watching. At points along the ribbon are many of the buildings and monuments which chart Leicester's history as a mediaeval town and as an industrial city. Much of the work which has transformed the Riverside was done by young people in the Riverside Community Programme Team (later Employment Training Team). The City Council's full-time wardens help to protect the Park and to foster interest in it among local school children and community groups.

The Riverside is an important home for wildlife with a large variety of plant species and an interesting range of birds and mammals. Water birds such as mallard, little grebe, and coot can be seen on most visits. The Riverside has also attracted more unusual species like short-eared owl and long-eared owl which both wintered in the Watermead area in 1991-92. As a habitat for wildlife the Riverside is a key element in the City Council's Ecology Strategy. The Strategy, published in 1989, set out the importance of the City's wildlife habitats and put forward policies for conserving them as the City changes.

The City Council's work on the Riverside won a major award from the European conservation organisation Europa Nostra in 1989 and, together with the Ecology Strategy, helped to spearhead Leicester's successful bid to be designated the first Environment City.

ABOVE AND TOP RIGHT Packhorse Bridge, Aylestone, 15th century

RIGHT Watermead Country Park: winter flooding

ABOVE Market Square, North Evington: Market Hall (now a Madressa), 1890; bandstand and square layout, 1982

UPPER RIGHT Police Station and Fire Station, 1899

LOWER RIGHT Asfordby Street

# 26
# *Improvement and Enterprise*

SOME PARTS of the City feel different: there are particular features which seem to be repeated or a peculiar layout or choice of building materials. This is often because an individual made a mark on the area. In North Evington the person was Arthur Wakerley, a property developer, reforming politician and architect. From the 1880s he bought land in the area around Spinney Hill Park, a locality scarred by clay and lime pits which were providing building materials to cater for Leicester's expansion. His aim was to build an industrial suburb of good quality houses, with factories, parks and entertainments all close at hand.

The centrepiece of this new community was to be North Evington Market Square. Wakerley designed the main buildings and this is where his personality begins to impose itself. His buildings had a distinctly flamboyant style. He particularly liked the kind of decoration found on buildings in the Netherlands and the Market Hall, built in 1890, has big curved Dutch gables and Dutch-derived *strapwork* decoration. Originally it contained a barber's shop, doctor's surgery, and coffee house (Wakerley was a keen opponent of the evils of alcohol). Nearby is the police station and fire station, built in 1899 in a similar style.

Today the Market Square is a very different place from the focal point planned by Wakerley. The market never really prospered and it closed in the 1940s. By the early 1980s the square was run down and neglected. An ugly concrete building had been built against the wall of Wakerley's Market Hall and the Market Place was being used as a car park for neighbouring factories. Then the City Council, through East Midlands Housing Association, commissioned the architects

RIGHT Strapwork and obelisk decoration, Market Hall

FAR RIGHT Painted glass in shopfront, Asfordby Street

LOWER FAR RIGHT Resources and Rehabilitation Centre, Gedding Road, 1986

Rod Hackney and Associates to design a scheme to open up the square and turn it back into the sort of public space which Wakerley had envisaged. Part of Atkinson Street was closed and incorporated into the square and a new building replaced the concrete addition to the Market Hall. Other buildings were cleaned and repaired and a bandstand built to act as a central feature of the new square.

There is another important respect in which the square has changed. The former works canteen for the Imperial Typewriter factory on the south side is now the Jam-e-Mosque. The Market Hall, which had been a constitutional club, is a Madressa: a Muslim school. The life of the square reflects the pattern of prayer and children's study. The mix of religious and ethnic groups is reflected in the steep streets around the square and in the local factories and shops.

Gwendolen Road was named after Arthur Wakerley's eldest daughter and many of the streets linking with it have names associated with the Wakerley family. Between Gedding Road (after Wakerley's house in Suffolk) and Margaret Road (after another daughter) Wakerley gave land to build housing and workshops for blind people. Royal Leicestershire Rutland and Wycliffe Society for the Blind still use the site and the buildings Wakerley designed for them. Again Wakerley indulges his taste for Dutch gables and other bold decoration, illustrated by the Wycliffe Hall and cottages on Gwendolen Road. The Blind Work Institute came later in 1922: with its tower, stonework and Tudor windows it looks a little like an English country house of the sixteenth century.

Six houses were built on Gedding Road for blind workers: they have carved door surrounds and herringbone woodwork in the doors. The pantiled porches resemble cottages in Suffolk from where the road name came. Before manufacture started in Britain pantiles were brought from Holland and Flanders in ships and used mainly on the eastern side of the country. The theme is taken up by the sweeping pantile roofs and bold pattern of windows in the Resources and Rehabilitation Centre built in 1986 to a design by the architects Douglas Smith Stimson Partnership.

Many of Wakerley's concerns were echoed and complemented by a younger Leicester contemporary, Harry Hardy Peach (1874~1936). Peach was interested in the principles of the Arts and Crafts movement and knew some of its leading figures. Although he admired and bought craft goods, like the furniture of Ernest Gimson, Peach's own aim was to produce, on an industrial basis, well designed and reasonably priced products for everyday use. In 1911 he founded the Dryad company, producing cane furniture, metal work (including architectural goods such as door handles), and handicraft materials and tools. Dryad became known worldwide and, by the 1930s, was the world's leading supplier of handicraft goods. The company had a shop in St Nicholas Circle which sold Dryad products and a wide range of pottery, glass, toys, and other items from around

TOP Gedding Road: houses for blind workers, c1915

FAR RIGHT Royal Leicestershire Rutland and Wycliffe Society for the Blind, Margaret Road, 1922

One of Wakerley's biggest achievements was not in town planning or designing prominent buildings, but in the design of a type of house to meet the desperate shortage of good housing after the First World War. Wakerley's solution was to build pairs of semi-detached houses sharing a chimney stack, roof ridge and water and gas pipe. The first Wakerley houses cost £299 each to build. They were used, with some variations on the basic design, all over Leicester and in other cities such as Glasgow and Belfast. There are Wakerley houses in Gedding Road. With adaptation to modern standards they still make attractive homes. Many have sadly lost original windows and doors, but there are examples of Wakerley houses which keep something like their original outward appearance in Linton Street off Evington Road. Care in the design and workmanship of small buildings makes a greater contribution to the well-being of a city and its people than the building of great monuments. Wakerley's modest, cheap, but distinctive houses are a product of Leicester in which the City can take pride.

RIGHT Wakerley houses in Linton Street, 1920s

BELOW RIGHT Wycliffe Hall, 1903

BELOW LEFT Remains of Harry Peach's lettering scheme uncovered during shopfront alterations at 114a London Road in 1995

the world. Harry Peach was an international figure with particularly strong links with designers and manufacturers in Germany. Through the Design and Industries Association he campaigned tirelessly for better design standards for manufactured goods.

Peach was equally energetic in his campaigns for a better environment in Leicester and around the country. With his friends and associates, notably Benjamin Fletcher (Head Master of Leicester School of Art), Percy Gee (radical heir to the Stead and Simpson shoe firm), William Pick of the hosiery firm, Sidney Gimson and other members of the Gimson family, he made Leicester one of the foremost cities in the *Town Tidying* movement which aimed to make an improvement in the appearance of British cities and in the quality of life enjoyed by their citizens. To this end Peach galvanised the Leicester institutions of which he was a member: the Literary and Philosophical Society, the Rotary Club, the Kyrle Society (forerunner of the present Civic Society), and the Leicestershire Footpaths Association. He campaigned to have unsightly advertisements removed from the streets of Leicester, particularly from London Road Station and the bridge parapet opposite. Harry Peach was known nationally for his crusades against litter: he encouraged Leicester Corporation to provide litter bins on the streets and on trams and buses.

Peach fought for decent schools and parks and advocated hygienic public lavatories and bus shelters with equal vigour. He had a strong interest in lettering and graphic design and produced a scheme for a row of shops on London Road (numbers 108-114a, opposite University Road), in which the uniform shopfronts were complemented by signs all in the same lettering style. These shops were featured in a Design and Industries Association publication as a model for the rest of the country to follow. Harry Peach and his friends also campaigned for the adoption of a scheme devised by Benjamin Fletcher to turn a derelict area beside the Castle and St Mary de Castro Church into gardens as a memorial to the dead of the Great War. This was the initiative that led to the laying out of Castle Gardens.

Although Harry Peach is not commemorated today by specific buildings or streets as are other figures mentioned, many of his concerns are echoed in this book. He made Leicester, for a time, a leader in the field of town improvement and we hope that, in some respects at least, the City has followed where Peach led.

# 27
# *High Street*

MANY TOWNS with a strong historic character have two points in common: they were built within a limited time span, usually a past period of prosperity, and they then drifted out of the economic mainstream. Leicester's High Street has had something of this. It is an historic street: the East Gate and West Gate of the Roman town were at opposite ends of the present

South side of High Street: redeveloped after 1902

TOP AND LOWER RIGHT 76-80 High Street, 1902-04, details of glazed terracotta (faience)

FAR RIGHT Lloyds Bank, 9 High Street, 1903-06

High Street. King James I and King Charles I stayed at a house called Lord's Place which stood near what is now the west entrance to the Shires. But, in 1902, much of the old High Street, including Huntingdon Tower, the last remnant of Lord's Place, was swept away to widen the street to take trams. The street today owes its character to the buildings that were put up after the widening. The fact that so many of them have survived is partly due to the position of the street a little outside the hub of the City Centre commercial area. For years High Street had mixed fortunes but recently, with the development of the Shires, the retail centre of gravity changed and interest in building and rebuilding has picked up.

The Edwardian rebuilding gave us a fine set of buildings in High Street. The group on the south side between St Nicholas Place and Carts Lane is particularly lively with a wildly varied skyline. The most original buildings are Numbers 76-86, built to Arthur Wakerley's design as the Coronation Building in 1902-04. They reflect the imperial confidence of Edwardian Britain. Roundels in coloured faience show animals representing parts of the Empire. Other panels show ships sailing out to trade with, or conquer, other countries. On the corner of Carts Lane 58 High Street has a helmet-like dome on top of a lighthouse tower which seems to provide a marine complement to the tiled advertisement for *Sea Breeze* headache cure.

Old photographs of High Street show a mass of advertisements and shop signs, many of them enormous by today's standards. The Edwardian builders and architects also made the buildings themselves advertisements for the business inside. Even

TOP LEFT TO RIGHT

Edwardian Baroque detail in High Street, post-1902

Sea Breeze advertisement, 60 High Street, c1902

76-80 High Street, detail

RIGHT Dutch gable and turret, 1902-03, now part of the Shires

so, the slightly overweight nude figures over the door of the Electric Theatre (now incorporated in rebuilt form into a shop frontage) surely could not have represented the films shown when the cinema was built in 1910, even if they encouraged customers.

Lloyd's Bank at Number 9, built in 1903-06, looks solid and dependable: a place to keep your money with confidence. Its design, by Chatwin and Son of Birmingham, owes much to the seventeenth century architect Inigo Jones who brought from Italy Classical architecture which was startlingly modern in its time. Close to the Clock Tower shops vied for customers' attention with a collection of spires, domes, turrets and gables. The Shires continues the tradition with its entrance arches and the corner turret at the western end of the scheme.

Today the upper floors are often the most interesting parts of buildings in the City Centre. Many ground floors, originally part of the overall design of the building, have been changed to conform to the corporate image of a shopping chain. Some designers have not properly considered the shopfront as an integral part of the appearance of the building and little thought has been given to the individual character of the building or the town. The obsession with corporate identity has done a great deal to take away the character of towns and cities. The damage which this lack of imagination and design skill has caused will take years

ABOVE Former Eastgates Coffee House, 1885 with ground floor refurbishment completed in 1996

TOP RIGHT Cathedral spire and shops at the junction of High Street and Silver Street: the latter designed by the Goddard practice in 1896 and one of the best of Leicester's corner buildings

RIGHT Edwardian shopfront, 60 High Street

to put right. At present planning consent is not normally needed for shop fascia signs unless they are lit. Changes in planning law to bring all external shop signs under control subject to planning policies, could make a vast improvement in our towns.

There is a beautifully kept shopfront at 60 High Street, near the junction with Carts Lane, with curved glass leading into the doorway and delicate wood and cast iron work. Even here the shopfront is spoiled by the tiled treatment of the adjoining ground floor. Over recent years the City Council has tried to encourage, often by offering grants, timber shopfronts of a design which harmonises with the upper floors of the building. There are some examples of this approach in High Street.

The Clock Tower is still in many ways the focal point of Leicester. It was designed by Joseph Goddard and built in 1868. Ketton limestone from Rutland was used with pink granite and marble columns. The style is Gothic with pointed arches and a mass of spiky turrets and *crockets* (carved decorative projections from the angles of spires etc.). Samuel Barfield, who carved stone decorations at Midland Bank in Granby Street and in Rutland Street, made the statues of famous figures from Leicester's history: Simon de Montfort,

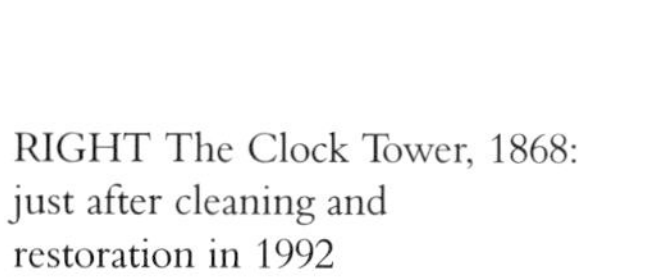

RIGHT The Clock Tower, 1868: just after cleaning and restoration in 1992

FAR RIGHT The Shires turret, 1991, and part of retained facade to Leicestershire Co-operative Society building, 1884

LOWER LEFT Entrance to The Shires, High Street 1994

LOWER RIGHT Statue of Sir Thomas White, the Clock Tower during restoration

William Wigston, Sir Thomas White, and Alderman Gabriel Newton. In 1992 local architects and engineers Pick Everard, chose the restoration of the Clock Tower as a project to mark their 125th anniversary, and made a substantial financial and professional contribution to the programme of cleaning and stonework restoration.

The architectural mood of High Street is rather jolly but at the corner of Eastgates and Church Gate is a reminder of a literally sober side to life in Victorian and Edwardian Leicester. The Eastgates Coffee House was one of a chain of similar institutions aimed at giving working men an alternative to the lure of the pubs. They were a part of the serious, reforming element in the life of Nonconformist Leicester. The architect Edward Burgess was involved in the coffee house movement and designed several of the buildings. They were ornate on the outside to attract customers who, on entering, found a spartan interior. The Eastgates building is in a rather Germanic style and is closely based on the Ossington Coffee House in Newark which was built just before it. When Eastgates Coffee House was built in 1885 it had a beautiful arched ground floor which suffered at the hands of retailers in the way we have already described. A modern arched design completed in 1996 helps to reunite the upper floors with the shopfront.

# 28
# *The Edwardians*

IN THE FIRST FOURTEEN YEARS of the twentieth century Leicester was still in the period of prosperity which had continued since the 1870s. The picture of the period presented by its buildings has two strands: one is the wealth and confidence illustrated by High Street; the other is the quiet and simple elegance of roads like Sykefield Avenue and Morland Avenue.

Morland Avenue, laid out 1904

TOP LEFT Morland Avenue: detail of roughcast render

TOP RIGHT Morland Avenue doorway

ABOVE LEFT Morland Avenue: front gate

ABOVE RIGHT Morland Avenue: bracket supporting bay roof

They give an incomplete impression of a town in which thousands of people still lived in slums although the Edwardians did build some good quality cheap housing. It is the large suburban houses, churches, shops and factories, which remain as the Edwardians' main contributions to the character of Leicester today.

Morland Avenue was laid out in 1904 by the architect Stockdale Harrison who also designed many of the houses. In the first decade of the twentieth century Harrison designed a number of houses in Leicester in styles influenced by the Arts and Crafts movement. Decoration is used very sparingly. The attractiveness of the houses depends on the materials used: mostly roughcast render and tiles for the prominent roofs and for covering parts of the walls, and on

RIGHT AND FAR RIGHT Morland Avenue, porches

LOWER RIGHT Morland Avenue, lead gutter

the irregular pattern of big gables facing the street. The cottage-like appearance which results is enhanced by the small-paned windows. The original windows are nearly all still intact or have been replaced by close copies. Doorways present visitors with an impression of the importance of the building and the people who live in it: most of the decoration of the Morland Avenue houses is concentrated on the doorways and porches supported on carved timber brackets or columns. The gables are stepped down the hill and views along the street softened by rows of delicate silver birch trees.

# PART FOUR

School of Engineering and Manufacture, De Montfort University

*Leicester was granted the title of City in 1919. The process of growth and change has become more controlled but the City of 1919 has been radically refashioned particularly in response to the growth of motor traffic. Leicester has become home to a diverse mixture of people of many different cultures.*

# 29
# *Recreation and Remembrance*

VICTORIA PARK was once the town racecourse. It became rather scruffy and down-at-heel, and was laid out as a park in 1883. The main land-mark buildings around the Park are from the twentieth century. Leicester University will be

FACING PAGE Victoria Park: the War Memorial, 1923

RIGHT Church of St James the Greater, London Road, 1899-1914

LOWER RIGHT Victoria Park

considered later - this chapter will concentrate on the northern side of the Park nearest to London Road.

Victoria Park is very different from the other late nineteenth century parks in the City. There was little attempt to create a picturesque landscape with ornamental trees, rockeries, or formal flower beds as there was at Abbey Park. The quality of Victoria Park lies in its size and openness, broken only by avenues of trees. It feels expansive and refreshing. On Sunday mornings the Park is colourful and active with football matches. A summer's evening sees Victoria Park alive with games of cricket. As dusk falls on a winter's afternoon the Park is at its most impressive, the buildings around the edge lit up and traffic, for once an asset, giving a sense of buzzing activity beyond the open space.

The London Road frontage has an impressive range of early nineteenth century, Victorian, and later houses. The main landmark is the Church of St James the Greater. Originally it was intended to be an even stronger accent with a soaring central tower, alas never

ABOVE Church of St James the Greater

TOP RIGHT Victoria Park

RIGHT The War Memorial, incised lettering

built, which would have been the most prominent building in Leicester in its time. St James the Greater was designed by the Goddard practice and Joseph Goddard's son, Henry Langton Goddard, travelled to Italy searching for ideas. He came back to design an Italian Renaissance style building in brick and stone with prominent towers overlooking the Park. The church has a serene interior with round arches in a style taken from the eleventh century Early Christian cathedral at Torcello near Venice. Building started in 1899 but was not fully completed until 1914.

The tragic events which began in 1914 were to give rise to the next landmark in Victoria Park. Leicester commissioned Sir Edwin Lutyens, regarded by many architects and historians as the finest British architect of the twentieth century, to design the memorial to the Leicester people killed in the Great War. Beside the tennis courts and football pitches, the tall, powerful arch is a dignified and sombre reminder of the impact of world history on one community.

Lutyens also designed the lodges and gates at the London Road entrance to the Park. They may be expected to form a grand vista culminating in the War Memorial but the Memorial is not directly in line with the gates and the intervening space is filled partly by a car park. Instead Peace Walk forms the formal approach up the hill to the Memorial.

RIGHT The War Memorial, stone flag under central arch

FAR RIGHT The War Memorial

LOWER LEFT Victoria Park Lodges and gates, 1931-33

LOWER RIGHT Victoria Park Lodge Number 1: the false quoins between the windows are a quirky feature typical of the work of the architect of the lodges, Sir Edwin Lutyens

Lutyens was a master at using Classical architecture in an individual and inventive way. The lodges are built simply enough in brick coated in stucco. But they are quite substantial bungalows whose bulk is broken down to keep them in proportion with the gates and to form a balanced composition when seen from London Road. Lutyens also divided the expanse of the long sides of the buildings in a typically quirky way by using *quoins* (blocks normally forming the corner of a building) where there is actually no corner.

Since 1913 Leicester people have been entertained, thrilled or inspired at De Montfort Hall. After his Leicester design, the architect, Shirley Harrison, won a competition to build a new concert hall in Edinburgh. That building, the Usher Hall, is much more lavish than the hall which Harrison designed for his home town. But De Montfort Hall is thought by many experts to have some of the best acoustic conditions for music in the country. A conversion scheme carried out in 1993-94, while not without controversy, has provided a flexible arena for many kinds of performance. Shirley Harrison's impressive Classical frontage with its formal gardens, completes the group of landmarks around Victoria Park.

TOP De Montfort Hall 1913 with bar extension 1994

ABOVE Nicholas Kraemer rehearses the City of Birmingham Symphony Orchestra for a concert at De Montfort Hall on 29th March 1996

RIGHT De Montfort Hall: balcony detail

BELOW De Montfort Hall: interior with City of Birmingham Symphony Orchestra

TOP AND ABOVE 317-355 Narborough Road, 1927-28

# 30
# *Home*

THE LOCAL AUTHORITY responded to the problem of poor housing as early as 1900 by building Leicester's first council houses in Winifred Street. In 1919 a Leicester man, Sir Tudor Walters, then Member of Parliament for Sheffield Brightside, produced a report on housing in Britain which set out new standards for public housing throughout the country. Chapter 26 has shown how Arthur Wakerley devised a cheap design for housing after the Great War.

In its development in South Braunstone in 1927 to 1928, the Corporation provided housing and a pleasant environment which must have been inspired by the ideas behind contemporary garden cities like Letchworth or model villages like Port Sunlight. The showpiece of the estate, and one of the landmarks of the City for visitors approaching from the M1 and M69, is the crescent formed by 317 to 355 Narborough Road. The architect for the Corporation, James Simpson Fyfe, designed the houses. His clerk of works was George Marshall who had a long career in the building industry in Leicester and who gave his name to Marshall Street, off Woodgate.

The houses were designed to look like a row of picturesque cottages. Traditional materials were used for the fronts: brick and render and clay plain tiles for the roofs. Three of the houses have big gables in timber, jointed and pegged using proper carpentry techniques. Windows have small panes and the houses have prominent chimney stacks.

Although the first tenants thought the houses a long way from the City, they found them spacious

RIGHT 317-355 Narborough Road

LOWER RIGHT 317-355 Narborough Road, timber detail

and comfortable with luxuries such as inside toilets. Some of the residents have been there for several decades and the crescent shows the benefits of their commitment to the area in the neatness of the houses and the well-planted front gardens.

Many of the City's council houses have been altered through the need to maintain them on tightly controlled budgets or the changing aspirations of tenants who buy their homes. But 317-355 Narborough Road have kept their essential character even though some alterations have been made. They make an important contribution to Leicester's quality through the work of their architect, the skills of the people who built them, and the care of the people who live in them. Most of all they represent the far-sightedness of a local authority which set out, in difficult times, not just to tackle a housing problem, but to provide something of real and lasting quality.

# 31
# *Thirties*

AT THE END of the First World War building costs rose enormously and the highly decorated and finely crafted Baroque buildings popular before 1914 were usually no longer affordable. At the same time new ideas were coming into Britain from America and the Continent, some of them brought by exiles from the turmoil in Central Europe. New building methods were being introduced. Modern styles favoured the honest expression of the materials and construction over ornament. Leicester grew in size with housing by private builders and large estates built by the Corporation. Industry and entertainments grew as well. Buses took over from trams giving the City a much

ABOVE RIGHT Window of house in St Barnabas Road

RIGHT Houses in Broadway Road, 1930s

FACING PAGE LEFT Lewis's tower, 1935-36

FACING PAGE RIGHT Doorway of house in Broadway Road

more flexible transport system. But the City Centre kept its nineteenth century shape: the widening of Charles Street was the biggest change together with the arrival of the first big-city department store - Lewis's.

The need for better community services was a strong influence on the architecture of the 1930s and this concern produced some very friendly buildings. Symington Prince and Pike, the architects of the library in St Barnabas Road and a similar building in Saffron Lane, must have been aware of contemporary styles of brick building in Holland and Scandinavia. A library in Stockholm, which has a big circular brick tower, might have been a particular influence on the Leicester libraries. The architects

would also have seen the London Underground station designed by Charles Holden at Arnos Grove, built in 1932. It has a big circular entrance hall which gives the building a form similar to that of the libraries. These influences apart, one version of the origin has it that Maurice Pike drew his ideas from the shapes of tobacco tins!

The St Barnabas Library was built in 1937. It is faced in traditional brown brick with a modern concrete porch and metal windows. Simple decoration in brick and curved corners help to give the building a welcoming appearance. Inside is the light and airy circular reading room with just a hint of Classical architecture in the columns. Neat fitted bookshelves complete a lovely design, carried out with skill by the bricklayers, joiners and other craftsmen.

Art Deco, a style of decoration which used angular and other geometrical forms, was very fashionable in the 1920s and 1930s. In Nelson Street the Goddards' factory (now the offices of Edge and Ellison) is Leicester's best example. Built in 1932 and designed by Bedingfield and Grundy, it is also an example of modern forms of construction: the lightweight glazed outside walls are attached to a frame of concrete or steel which also carries the weight of the roof and the floors. Everywhere there are Art Deco features: in the pattern formed by the aluminium frame to the outer panels, in the stonework, and in the lead gutters and downpipes.

RIGHT Goddards' factory, Nelson Street, 1932, now in use as offices

BELOW Goddards' factory, details

FACING PAGE
TOP LEFT St Barnabas Library, 1937, exterior from French Road

LOWER LEFT St Barnabas Library, interior

LOWER RIGHT St Barnabas Library, detail of window and brickwork

Around the City are a number of Art Deco bus shelters with chevron patterns in the windows. There are examples in Narborough Road, Western Boulevard, Fosse Road North, Western Park and Humberstone Park. The pride in public services which these solid and stylish buildings express seems to contrast with many bus shelters today which are little more than advertisement hoardings with a roof.

Charles Street is the most complete 1930s street. It is often overlooked because it is so busy and because it is on the edge of the City Centre shopping area. But it is worth looking above the shopfronts in Charles Street. It is an old street, but few buildings survive from the time before its widening in 1932 which aimed to take through traffic from London to the north-west out of Granby Street and Gallowtree Gate.

TOP Varying styles of 1930s architecture in Charles Street: left to right (Rutland Street); The Queens pub, Georgian; 118, simplified Classical; 120 and 122, Georgian; Cherub factory, simplified Classical; 132-144, Modern; the Spread Eagle pub, Georgian (Church Street). In the foreground plant tubs dubbed 'Beckett's Buckets' after former City Surveyor, John L Beckett.

FAR RIGHT Attenborough House, formerly Municipal Offices, opened 1938

Some of the buildings on the east side between Rutland Street and Church Street have Classical overtones, but they show how Classical forms were used in a simplified way in the 1930s. Number 118 (next to the Queens pub) won a design award for its architects, Symington Prince and Pike again, in 1933. The original columns on the ground floor were later taken out. There is still just a suggestion of Classical detail between the arched windows and a touch of Art Deco in the wavy lines cast into the metal panels in the window openings. There is Classical detail in the big Cherub factory as well. Next to that is a building (now occupied by the AA) which seems to be more modern and which was altered and extended upwards in 1971. Decoration was reduced to bands of brick with long horizontal windows giving the building a rather flat appearance compared with the upward-looking vertical accents of its neighbours in the street. The pubs in Charles Street are all mock-Georgian in style, even where they use 1930s materials such as metal windows.

What is now Attenborough House was built as Municipal Offices and marked the growth of Corporation services and a need for offices outside the Victorian

RIGHT Attenborough House, with FAR RIGHT Mural paintings in Attenborough House lobby illustrating the benefits of electricity: the municipal electricity undertaking originally occupied part of the building.

Town Hall. A competition was held for the design which was won by Barnish and Silcock of Liverpool. The building was faced with hard white Portland stone, the approved material for official buildings of

TOP LEFT Four Winds clock by Albert Pountney, 1955-59, Alliance and Leicester Building Society, Charles Street

TOP RIGHT Bus Shelter, Narborough Road, 1930's

ABOVE Police Headquarters, Charles Street, 1933, architect: Noel Hill

the time. But the Spanish tiles on the roof would look more at home on a suburban house and the decorated metal grilles over the doors and windows also help to make the building a little friendlier. The metal windows and flagpoles are derived from details of Karl-Marx-Hof, a pioneering housing scheme in Vienna.

Nearby is the Alliance and Leicester building, designed for the Leicester Temperance Building Society by Pick Everard Keay and Gimson and built in 1955-59. The Four Winds clock on the central tower was the work of Albert Pountney, eminent both as a sculptor and as a teacher and administrator at Leicester Polytechnic.

Leicester's best known, and perhaps best loved, thirties building is Lewis's tower, built in 1935-36 to the design of G. de C. Fraser. Even with taller buildings to compete with it the elegance of Lewis's tower ensures that it remains one of the features of the City Centre skyline. When it was built it must have brought a note of metropolitan glamour to the small scale Leicester of the 1930s. Lewis's store was demolished in 1995 and the tower now forms the centrepiece for a new shopping development and square.

# 32
# *Garden City*

LEICESTER has its own garden city at Humberstone with a history rooted in a movement which built towns like Letchworth and Welwyn. But Letchworth gave its name to a road on the opposite side of the City which looks a little like some of the streets of the same era in the Hertfordshire town. Letchworth Road is tree-lined with large detached houses. The

Letchworth Road, 1920s/1930s

TOP LEFT Summer Hill, Letchworth Road, 1909

AND TOP RIGHT Letchworth Road

ABOVE Letchworth Road area from Western Park

houses are individually designed but mix Georgian details with others derived from traditional cottage building: the influence of the Arts and Crafts movement was still evident. The houses also share a range of materials: brick, render and timber, with roofs in tiles, Welsh slate, or occasionally Swithland slate. Although each house is different the street has an overall pattern formed by bays, gables and chimneys, dormers and porches.

Some of the houses were built before 1914 but most date from the 1920s or 1930s. By this time their fairly well-off owners would have needed space for the car and most of the houses have garages. The garage doors fit neatly into the appearance of the houses: they are made of wood and have windows of a pattern to echo the rest of the house.

TOP LEFT TO RIGHT
Letchworth Road
Westfield Road
St Anne's Church: *tin tabernacle*: prefabricated church building used as church rooms

ABOVE St Anne's Church, 1934, from Westfield Road

ABOVE RIGHT Green Gables, Westhill Road

On a dramatic site on the top of the hill on Westfield Road is St Anne's Church, built in 1934 to serve the growing community in the area. The previous chapter has shown how, after 1918, Classical styles were stripped-down to accommodate a steep rise in building costs. At St Anne's, Gothic was reduced in a similar way to simple pointed arches and patterns formed in brick. The architect was Arthur Bryan of Leicester. Despite the general severity of the building he did splash out a little on stonework for the windows which have tracery in a variety of patterns based on the Decorated style. The building was never fully finished but St Anne's provides an impressive focal point for the pleasant suburban streets around it.

TOP LEFT Letchworth Road

TOP RIGHT St Anne's Church, east end

ABOVE Westfield Road

# 33
# *Estates*

AFTER THE SECOND WORLD WAR the need for new and better homes remained just as urgent as it had been in the 1920s and 1930s. The Corporation carried out an enormous programme of council house building in the 1950s of which there is space for only one example in this book.

At Evington, in the estate based on Cordery Road, the Corporation's architects and builders produced housing in an environment as pleasant as any in the City. The cost of new council housing was closely controlled by the Government and building materials were scarce. There was little money available for

Cordery Road, junction with Main Street Evington, 1952-53

decorative work and the houses are mainly in inexpensive brick with concrete tiled roofs and metal windows. But the site had many mature trees which enhanced the new development and economy did not prevent thoughtful design from creating attractive groups of houses and streets. This is particularly so at the junction of Cordery Road and Main Street where a group of old people's bungalows wraps around the corner with staggered frontages and rooflines nestling under a big beech tree. Cordery Road has been cared for and has aged well. The brick now looks pleasantly mellow and the concrete tiles are softened by lichen growth. Many of the front gardens are very well planted and looked after.

Across Evington Park is a different approach to designing housing and to providing housing originally to rent. Douglas Smith Stimson Partnership designed

ABOVE AND RIGHT Aldgate Avenue, 1950

TOP LEFT Cordery Road, topiary

TOP RIGHT Falmouth Road Estate and Carrick Point, 1972

ABOVE Medium-rise flats and maisonettes, 1972: trees planted as young stock have matured to become an important feature of the estate

the Falmouth Road estate in the early 1970s for Leicester Co-ownership Housing Society No.2. The small site contains a mix of individual houses in short terraces, flats in four storey blocks with access via staircases, and a fourteen storey building. The tower block, Carrick Point, is perhaps the most interesting element. It contains only small flats for single people and couples without children but the estate as a whole has a balanced community. Carrick Point is built in structural brickwork, the weight of the floors and roof being supported on the brick walls rather than on a steel or concrete frame. The structure derives strength from the many recesses and angles in its plan which also give interest to the elevations of the building. The trees, planted as young stock when the housing was first built, have now grown to become an important feature of the estate.

The skyline of Carrick Point is now crowned with a bulky aerial to serve mobile telephones: an example of the not altogether welcome impact of improvements in communications on the appearance of our towns and countryside.

# 34
# *Three Towers*

LEICESTER UNIVERSITY is one of the salient features of the City skyline. In its relatively short life the University has brought nationally known architects to the City and has given Leicester a landmark recognised all over the world. The compact University site offers a catalogue of changing architectural styles over the past 40 years.

The story began in 1919 when Thomas Fielding Johnson gave to Leicester a building of 1836 designed by William Parsons as a lunatic asylum. Fielding Johnson also donated land around the building and the Leicester Leicestershire and Rutland College was opened there in 1921. By 1926 it had become a university college and the

University of Leicester received its charter in 1957.

The buildings of the early 1950s take their theme from the Fielding Johnson Building with its rather stern Classical style. A move towards more modern buildings began in 1957 when the architect Sir Leslie Martin drew up a master plan for the development of land to the north-east of the then existing site which the Corporation had sold to the University. The main science buildings occupy this site between University Road, Victoria Park, and Peace Walk. These buildings help to shape the intimate atmosphere of the University. Although the white tiled Adrian Building is more aggressive, most of the buildings on this part of the campus are faced in warm yellow brick and have dark horizontal bands of windows. They are grouped around a pleasant series of courtyards with as much thought given to the spaces in which the buildings stand as to the buildings themselves. The quality of these spaces is maintained by good planting and grounds maintenance.

The Engineering Building, begun in 1959, is much more individual than this well-ordered collection. This is the building which, more than any other, rep-

FACING PAGE Leicester University with spire of Holy Trinity Church and clock tower of Lancaster Road Fire Station

BELOW Fielding Johnson Building, 1836, and *Souls* by Helaine Blumenfeld

RIGHT Leicester University, west side of campus

LOWER LEFT New Building 1995

LOWER RIGHT Leicester University: Astronomical Clock, 1989, on Rattray Lecture Theatre

FACING PAGE LEFT AND RIGHT Leicester University Engineering Building, 1959-63

resents Leicester in the minds of people interested in architecture throughout the world. The site presented to the architects, James Stirling and James Gowan, had an awkward shape. To add to the problems, the various activities involved in teaching and researching in engineering demanded different building forms. The raked floor of the lecture theatre is expressed on the outside and has a little spiral staircase for students coming late to lectures. The crystalline form of the workshop block is dictated by the need to light the delicate machines inside it from the north despite the awkward orientation of the site. Each element is shaped by the purpose it serves and the whole composition is an intriguing interplay of angles and volumes. The building echoes both the red brick of Leicester and the architecture of some of its factory buildings. Although parts of the Engineering Building are faced in red brick or tiles, the gravity-defying underside of the lecture theatre and the translucence

of the tower, evident even after it was re-glazed, depend on the use of steel and concrete construction.

The two other towers followed over the next decade. The Charles Wilson Building, designed by Denys Lasdun and built in 1962-67, has upper storeys forming a striking sculpture of tall concrete blocks and boxes. The Attenborough Building, by Ove Arup Associates, which followed in 1968-70, provides a more conventional foil for its two neighbours, its slightly angled windows giving an emphasis on pattern and texture rather than a dramatic silhouette.

The next big building was the Library, the work of the architects Castle Park Dean and Hook, built in 1971-74. Its front face is in brown reflective glass, a treatment much used in the 1970s particularly where it was important to fit a building into an existing group. Outside, the sculpture *Four Fold* by Stephen Collingbourne, echoes the angular forms of the buildings around it.

By the 1980s the architectural fashions which had influenced the Library had changed. In 1983 the Castle Park practice designed the Computer/Bio Centre on the site at the junction of Mayor's Walk and University Road. Its function is very different from that of the Library and the site had been a pleasant grassed and planted area before the Centre was built. Now that the shrub planting has matured the low building seems to crouch on its site, growing out of the grassy

ABOVE
The Richard Attenborough Centre for Disability and the Arts 1997

TOP RIGHT Library with reflections of Attenborough Building

LOWER RIGHT Computer Bio Centre Building, 1983

slope around it. The brickwork, mainly yellow, is used in a decorative way with red brick at the corners and around the openings. The big low roofs need a very light and impermeable metal covering, and huge rainwater heads and downpipes collect the water that runs off them. The Computer/Bio Centre was one of the first buildings in which the City Council's planners negotiated the inclusion of facilities for wheelchair users.

So how did the story continue into the 1990s? The next big building at Leicester University was the New Building for arts and social sciences, opened in 1995. Its architects are the successors to the Castle Park practice and they brought the story back to its beginning by designing a beautifully detailed Classical building to set beside William Parsons' asylum of 1836.

This relatively conservative design has not meant a retreat from the University's commitment to architectural innovation. The Richard Attenborough Centre on Lancaster Road, completed in 1997, combines glass, brick and timber in a Modern design of stunning clarity and simplicity by Ian Taylor of Bennett Associates. The tall glass fins which reflect light into the centre of the building are a key feature and give the building a dramatic, luminous quality when it is lit up after dark. The Centre's work encourages participation in the arts especially by people with disabilities.

Space science is one of the areas of study for which Leicester University is best known in the academic world. This discipline promises to provide the next chapter in the development of the main campus and, the City hopes, a public Space Centre elsewhere in Leicester that could mark the Millennium with a piece of breathtaking architecture.

RIGHT Leicester University: Library, 1971-74, and *Four Fold* by Stephen Collingbourne

BELOW Leicester University from Victoria Park: left to right, Engineering Building, 1959-63; Attenborough Building, 1968-70; and Charles Wilson Building, 1962-67.

# 35
# *High Rise*

LEICESTER has not always kept up with fashions in architecture and planning and this has often been to the City's advantage. There was never a very full commitment to high rise buildings, either for housing or for offices. So when high rise became associated with housing problems, windy and featureless city streets, and the excesses of the speculative property industry, Leicester had relatively little cause for concern compared with many other cities. Some high rise buildings did appear in Leicester in the 1960s and 1970s and there was some truth in the negative associations. But valid concern with the bad aspects of high-rise obscured many of its benefits.

ABOVE View north down London Road hill: Peat House in the centre, Arnhem House on the left

RIGHT The City from Western Park

Tower blocks were built at St Matthew's, St Peter's and at Rowlatts Hill for housing. Whatever the social and management problems tower blocks can give rise to as family housing, they can offer reasonable homes for single people and couples. Offices are a more suitable use for tower blocks and high office buildings, and in one case a telephone exchange, have given accents to the City Centre skyline in the decades since 1960.

From a distance, it is high buildings which now tend to signal where a city centre is: the view of the centre of Birmingham from the M6 for example, or, to a lesser extent, the view of Leicester's City Centre from the M1. Streets within the City Centre most dominated by high buildings are Humberstone Gate, and Charles Street where the view to the south is closed by the Postal Headquarters building. This is one of the most simple and restrained of Leicester's tower blocks. It relies for its visual effect on size and simple block-like shapes. The strips of window and concrete facing panel are equally elementary, but the details have been carefully designed and, unusually for a concrete building in the English climate, the Postal

BELOW
Left to right: St John's Chambers (former Church of St John the Divine, 1853-54, converted 1988-89), St John's House, Arnhem House (Peat House behind), Elizabeth House, Postal Headquarters

RIGHT St John's House, 1974, East Street / South Albion Street

FAR RIGHT Elizabeth House, 1976-77, London Road / Campbell Street

LOWER FAR RIGHT Postal Headquarters, 1971-72, Charles Street

Headquarters has weathered well. The building was designed in 1971-72 by the Property Services Agency.

Five years later architect John Middleton tackled a very different problem on the neighbouring site fronting London Road, designing Elizabeth House as a single persons' housing scheme. Concrete and glass dominate this building also but the bulk is broken up by recessed dark panels and modelling of the faces of the building. The surface of the concrete is ribbed and textured to provide a series of shadow lines and to soften its appearance.

On the other side of London Road the pattern is rather different. It was begun in 1974 by the Leeds architects Fletcher Ross and Hickling. They designed St John's House as part of a larger development on the same theme, but only one building was completed. The mass of St John's House is broken down by complex variations in height and by the splayed design of

RIGHT Elizabeth House and Postal Headquarters

FAR RIGHT Arnhem House, 1988-90, London Road / Waterloo Way, detail

the corners. The materials chosen were important: brown tinted glass and brown brick with a hard, reflective outer surface.

St John's House offered a high building which, with its less formal shape and brick facing, was perhaps more obviously popular than something like the Postal Headquarters. The rest of the site was a car park for over a decade until the resolution of boundaries after road building provided the conditions for two new buildings to go ahead. The site provides the first glimpse of Leicester for visitors arriving by train and is on an important road junction. The planning brief prepared by the City Council called for a gateway to the City Centre. Two firms of architects and their corporate clients responded by designing buildings which frame and give new features to the view down the hill on London Road and across the City towards Charnwood.

London architects, Frederick Gibberd Coombes and Partners designed Arnhem House, begun in 1988, as a cluster of brick-clad towers of varying heights, each with its own tiled pyramid roof. The height is stepped down towards the flats which now fill the former church of St John the Divine, until the 1970s the tallest building in the area. With its picturesque skyline and simple brickwork decoration, Arnhem House could hardly be more different from the Postal Headquarters as an approach to designing large buildings. The last building in the group is Peat House, also

ABOVE Arnhem House

TOP RIGHT Peat House, 1988-90, London Road / East Street

LOWER RIGHT Peat House and Elizabeth House

built in 1988. It is really too small to be considered high-rise but it carries on the picturesque theme of Arnhem House and echoes Victorian Leicester buildings. It is clad in an orange-red brick and has horizontal bands or *string courses* in creamy white brick. The architects, Douglas Marriot Worby Robinson, also from London, introduced colour in the blue window frames, panelling and railings. A big pyramid-roofed tower frames the view into Granby Street.

Modern styles, brought to Britain from the USA and Europe in the 1930s, were predominant in architecture, particularly for large buildings, until the 1970s. The group of buildings around London Road Station charts a move away from the automatic choice of a single style. They show that large buildings can be decorative elements in the street scene and can reflect and enhance the existing character of a town or city.

# 36
# *Citizens*

ALMOST EVERYONE born in Leicester must be descended from people who came from another country to make their home in Britain. They differ only in the number of generations for which their families or their ancestors have called Leicester home. Members of ethnic minorities, in building families and communities, have made an outstanding contribution to all aspects of the City's life. This contribution is illustrated throughout the book. But the diversity of ethnic and cultural groups is a key part of Leicester's character today: it is worth focusing specifically on the elements of the City's environment that express the aspirations of ethnic minority citizens.

ABOVE The Jain Centre, Oxford Street, converted from Congregational chapel begun 1983, interior

RIGHT Welcome banner, Moat Community College

Religion is an important aspect of life in the City and the various faiths have a multi-faith council to develop a dialogue among them and to foster mutual respect and tolerance. Work is in hand to build a multi-faith centre to give a tangible expression to these ideals. Religious festivals like Diwali, Eid, and Vaisakhi, and more secular events like the Caribbean Carnival, are part of the rhythm of life in Leicester. Some of these events have an impact on streets and buildings: the Diwali lights in Belgrave Road and the decorated doorsteps of the nineteenth century terraced houses nearby, for example.

Religion is also expressed in the use of buildings. Schools, houses, factories, and Christian churches have changed their uses to become mosques, temples, or gurdwaras. Sometimes the alteration is minimal: there is little outward sign of the use of the Jam-e-Mosque in Asfordby Street except the sign and the sight of the large

TOP LEFT Diwali celebrations in Belgrave Road

TOP RIGHT AND ABOVE Leicester Caribbean Carnival, 1992

LOWER RIGHT Jam-e-Mosque, Asfordby Street

RIGHT The Nishan Sahib: the saffron flag, unfurled for special festivals, which marks a Sikh gurdwara, Guru Nanak Gurdwara, Holy Bones

FAR RIGHT TOP AND LOWER Shree Swaminarayan Temple, Loughborough Road: a late nineteenth century house converted to a Hindu temple in 1991

BELOW Conduit Street Mosque, begun 1988

clock through the window. The main indication of the gurdwara in Holy Bones is the tall saffron flag outside, unfurled for special festivals, although the gurdwara community have aspirations to provide a more prominent expression of their faith and traditions.

Other religious buildings have made a very clear impact. The mosque on Sparkenhoe Street adds a golden fibreglass dome to the City's skyline. The Shree Swaminarayan Temple in Loughborough Road has built a tall sikhar, domes and a carved wooden porch onto the front of a late Victorian house. The Shree Jalaram Prathana Mandal adds traditional Hindu architectural motifs to the street scene in Narborough Road and has spectacular wall paintings inside. Most ambitious of all is the Jain Centre in Oxford Street. A Congregational church built in 1865 was transformed almost beyond recognition by marble and other stone sculpted in India to make one of the most ornate and remarkable buildings in the City.

ABOVE RIGHT Mural painting in Games Room at Moat Community College

RIGHT Leicester's Chinese community celebrate the arrival of the Year of the Rooster, Beaumont Leys, January 1993

FAR RIGHT Jain Centre, Oxford Street

The creative imagination of members of ethnic minorities and the diversity of their cultures has been expressed in art work at Moat Community College, in calligraphy over the lintels of houses, and in mural paintings around the City.

The ethnic minority communities represent a vast range of cultures, languages and religions and they have contributed many new sights to Leicester's streets. In some ways these new elements reflect aspects of historic Leicester. The colour and bustle of Belgrave Road Shopping Centre calls to mind Victorian photographs of busy shopping streets, not least Belgrave Road itself. The sober, industrious, and deeply religious community in North Evington must be close to the vision which Arthur Wakerley had for his new suburb. Wakerley, who drew freely on styles and ideas from abroad in his architecture, would surely have enjoyed the varied sights and sounds that Leicester's ethnic minority citizens have brought to today's City.

RIGHT Mural paintings by Mr B.J. Soni in Shree Jalaram Prathana Mandal, Narborough Road 1995

LOWER RIGHT Shree Jalaram Prathana Mandal and spire of Church of the Martyrs

BELOW Street mural in Wood Hill

# 37
# *New Horizon*

PLANNING, through a series of laws and regulations laid down by Parliament, was introduced in the twentieth century, most notably by the Town and Country Planning Act of 1947. But town planning, in the sense of seeking a rational arrangement of uses of land within a limited space, is much older. The Romans laid out their town on a square grid pattern with spaces allocated to the forum, temple, and baths. The development of the Southfields shows a predetermined plan. Terraced housing throughout the City in the later nineteenth century was laid out according to space standards set down in bye-laws. During the twentieth century both population and the number of households has grown and the speed

Amadis Close, 1981-82

of change in technology, particularly in transport, has increased. The planning system aims to make sure that these changes are catered for in a way which causes minimum damage to the environment and makes the best use possible of one of Britain's most scarce and valuable resources: land. For the most part planning is concerned with knitting changes into the existing pattern of towns, villages and the countryside. But sometimes it is necessary to plan for large scale new development on a site which has not previously been built up. In Leicester Beaumont Leys was a case in point.

Beaumont Leys had been owned by the Corporation since the end of the nineteenth century when it was bought as land for sewage treatment. This introduced restrictions on the use of part of the land which was an important consideration when plans for developing it were drawn up. The growth in population and the number of households was foreseen in the 1960s. Schools, leisure centres, and shops would be needed to serve these people. The City also needed space to expand its industrial base to strengthen the local economy and to provide jobs. The development of Beaumont Leys was seen as a way to meet these needs in a properly planned way, using the land owned by the City Council for the future growth of the City.

FAR RIGHT Eskdale Close, 1976-77

The first plan was drawn up in 1967 under the supervision of City Planning Officer Konrad Smigielski. It reflected ideas of the time for new towns in other parts of the country with a clearly defined main transport route and buildings marking this route and other landmarks. A monorail was an early feature of the plan and the whole approach aimed to provide a strong, futuristic, three-dimensional design for the new development.

By the time the Smigielski plan came to be looked at again in the 1970s the Council's ideas about planning Beaumont Leys, and the City as a whole, had changed. There was a greater awareness of the inter-dependence of land uses and transport and of the economic and social consequences of change in the environment. It was also doubtful whether the Council could rigidly control the development to produce a successful township of the type foreseen by the planners of ten years earlier. The population target was reduced giving more space for houses with gardens rather than the high proportion of flats originally intended. The loop road was replaced by a looser figure-of-eight which could give good access to public transport.

From the start it was envisaged that housing areas would be divided up into distinct plots, and that architects and developers would give an individual identity to each of these small areas.

Inevitably with a development taking place over a long period, progress on the ground has been affected by the

TOP AND ABOVE Eskdale Close

peaks and troughs of the housing market. Each phase has reflected the fashions of its time, and this has perhaps helped to achieve the varied character desired at the outset. Apart from changing architectural styles, the most noticeable difference between the various housing areas at Beaumont Leys is in their layout and, in particular, in the design and pattern of the roads.

An early phase of housing at Beaumont Leys used a *Radburn* layout (named after a pioneering scheme in New Jersey USA) in which houses face onto pedestrian paths which are completely separated from the roads. This did not prove popular and soon a more conventional approach was adopted in which most houses face estate roads and footways run alongside these roads. Since the late 1970s great efforts have been made to give housing estates a less bland appearance. This has been achieved by designing more informal road layouts with more interesting grouping of the houses, by generous planting of trees and shrubs, and by using better materials, such as small paving blocks, for the ground surface. More recently, safety has been improved by controlling the speed of vehicles with measures such as ramps and chicanes. It is equally important to provide open space and play areas properly integrated into housing layouts. Existing trees and hedgerows and older buildings like farmhouses help to give new housing areas a maturity and sense of belonging they may otherwise take years to acquire.

Eskdale Close was developed by the North British Housing Association in 1976-77 to a design by Barton Willmore Partnership. It is a mixture of flats and houses on a gentle south-facing slope next to Beaumont Walk, a pleasant footpath which winds through the southern part of Beaumont Leys. Details of doors and windows are simple and the quality of the scheme lies in the layout which creates a series of small courtyards, some with mature trees protected while building took place.

Trees also help to give an established, village-green, atmosphere to Amadis Close, developed by the City Council in 1981-82. The appearance of the houses themselves is slightly less plain

TOP Eskdale Close and Beaumont Walk

ABOVE Eskdale Close

TOP RIGHT AND LOWER RIGHT Paterson Close, 1984

ABOVE, TOP RIGHT, AND FAR RIGHT Halley Close, 1985

than at Eskdale Close with a mixture of brick, concrete pantiles, plain tiles, and timber cladding used for the outside finishes.

At Paterson Close, built for the City Council in 1984, materials include roughcast render, giving a distinctly Scottish quality to the range of flats backing onto Bennion Road. This development also makes interesting use of angles: tall windows break the eaves line forming slopes running counter to the main roof slopes, and tops of chimney stacks tilt to echo the roof.

In 1985 John Middleton designed Halley Close for De Montfort Housing Society. The architect deliberately set out to create a Leicestershire village, achieving by design what, in a real village, would take centuries to develop. Details like the small-paned windows are carefully observed but the scheme was built to a tight budget and the informal atmosphere is achieved by skilful design and mixing of a small range of materials and components. The layout is complemented by planting and by outside details like the granite copings in the boundary walls and attractive front gates. The approach is totally dif-

RIGHT AND BELOW
Brackenfield Chase, 1988

RIGHT Charnwood Forest horizon from Astill Lodge Road

BELOW

LEFT Brackenfield Chase

CENTRE AND RIGHT Charnwood Oaks, 1991

ferent from the disciplined geometry of the 1967 Master Plan.

The names which developers give to their individual sites often seem to be intended to give a promise of rural life to potential buyers. At Brackenfield Chase a

ABOVE RIGHT Monarch Knitting Machinery (UK), 1981, Boston Road

RIGHT Artisan Press: simple and powerful signs, 1979

BOTTOM RIGHT
PDI Group offices and factory, Boston Road, 1987-88

scheme designed by Barry Beesley Design for Balfour Beatty takes the village idea further even than Halley Close. The houses are large and aimed at relatively prosperous buyers. The scheme is on the City boundary close to Thurcaston and the design looks outside the City with a mixture of materials and details loosely based on cottage architecture. The large houses and generous space for parking give a much more spacious village layout than Halley Close: more reminiscent of a designed estate village like Edensor, on the Chatsworth estate in Derbyshire, than of a village which has grown over centuries. The most striking feature of Brackenfield Chase is the use of reed thatch to roof some of the houses. Thatch would once have been the most common roofing material for small houses in Leicester. There are now few thatched buildings in the City, although villages around have plenty. Its use at Brackenfield Chase, while a little quaint, is a reminder that Leicester forms part of the character of a larger area stretching outside the administrative boundary.

Nearby at Charnwood Oaks, Best Homes in 1991 created a different type of scheme for starter homes. The range of materials and details is very limited and doors and windows are standardised. The houses are laid out, at least to the main access roads, in broken lines giving pleasantly informal but skilfully-designed, coherent street frontages. At the moment some of the houses look out over open fields but planning policy for the adjoining sites will try to achieve a complementary design to give an interesting and distinctive street scene.

Among industrial buildings at Beaumont Leys, the most dominant is Walker's Crisps. But two earlier buildings on Boston Road, Artisan Press and Monarch Knitting Machinery (UK) Ltd., both by the Douglas Smith Stimson Partnership, better represent good industrial architecture. The buildings reflect the planning policy for the industrial area which called for a limited range of materials. Brown brick and dark brown windows and cladding were chosen and both buildings have an impressive, long, low profile. Another feature of both is their signs which form strong projecting blocks designed as an integral part of the architecture of the building. They show that a few powerful and well-designed signs are more effective than adding clutter to a building in an attempt to advertise.

The Beaumont Centre, built in 1983-84, provides shops and facilities such as a leisure centre for Beaumont Leys and for the whole City. The shopping area, designed by Gordon White and Hood, is grouped around a square and a market. Close to the shopping centre is the bold angular shape of Christ the King ecumenical church, which stands beside the leisure centre's flume. Other buildings, including the NSPCC Training Centre, are architecturally linked by red brick and big pantile roofs. But these buildings have yet to relate effectively to each other and they are separated from housing areas by extensive car parks and busy access roads. Perhaps the real theme which ties all the various elements of Beaumont Leys together is the rugged horizon and the changing moods of nearby Charnwood Forest.

ABOVE The Tower climbing wall 1995, Leys Leisure Centre

RIGHT Christ the King ecumenical church, Beaumont Centre, 1982-84

# 38
# *Shopping*

TRADING is one of the main reasons why towns exist; some towns were founded and continue to live solely as centres where people come together to buy and sell goods. Shopping is one of the most important and controversial subjects of concern to local councils in carrying out their planning functions. But most City Centre shops in the past developed where the traders thought they could make a living, often without any overall plan. This has given us the mixture of size and type of shop we are used to in the City Centre.

ABOVE The Shires opened, 1991

RIGHT Silver Arcade, 1899

ABOVE AND TOP RIGHT
Silver Arcade

LOWER FAR RIGHT
St Martin's Square, 1982-85

Today new shops are often in large developments, all or partly under cover and with large car parks. There is nothing new in providing a single building containing a number of shops. Silver Arcade was built in 1899 and designed by the architect Amos Hall. It has small shops on four levels inside with Baroque stone frontages to Silver Street and Cank Street. The interior is resplendent with decorative balustrades, lanterns and a frieze of rather roly-poly cherubs whose faces also appear carved in the stonework on the outside. The Arcade was refurbished in 1996 and the shops which occupy it today seem to echo the eccentricities of the design. It is a place for buying sought- after second hand books, clothes from some of the more specialised branches of the fashion trade, or a self-tie bow tie.

St Martin's Square caters for specialist shops in a different way. It was developed between 1982 and 1985 partly on land which had been derelict for many years. Some charming buildings on the street frontages were lost but a great deal was gained. The scheme, designed by Nicol Thomas Viner Barnwell for Teesland Development Company, set out to re-create the informal, random appearance provided by the demolished buildings. St Martin's Square reflects the market town aspect of Leicester's character. Small shops are loosely grouped around a central open space with arches through to the older streets outside. Some may feel

RIGHT St Martin's Square from St Martin's

LOWER RIGHT St Martin's Square, part of late-Victorian Jacobean style shopfront, previously located in Market Place South

that the scheme tries too hard to be pretty, with moulded timber shopfronts, decorative ironwork over the arch to St Martin's, clock tower and bandstand. But the quality of the design does not rely solely on decoration. The walkway from Cank Street, peeling away from the line of the street, and the narrow entrance through the arch from Silver Street opening into wider spaces, seek to provide by skilful design some of the pleasure of walking through an old town. The bricks, tiles and slates, are carefully chosen to blend with the older buildings around rather than to impose the new development on the City Centre in a showy way.

The Shires, opened in 1991, reflects the character of Leicester on the outside and its effect on High Street has been mentioned in Chapter 27. Inside, the architects, Chapman Taylor and Partners of London, deliberately tried to create something different and

TOP LEFT St Martin's Square from Cank Street

ABOVE The Shires

succeeded in giving the City a new space. The interior is spacious, light and airy. Its use of colour and Classically-based details reflects something of the Edwardian flamboyance of the High Street outside.

The success of the Shires led to its extension to Church Gate in 1994, giving extra shopping space and access to the scheme from a busy City Centre thoroughfare. The architects chose a different design theme for the exterior, using white metal cladding and glass to give a clean, sheer and totally modern frontage to the street.

The Shires was part of a national trend in city centre shopping both in the overall concept and in the design. Leicester must constantly respond to change if it is to attract shoppers from a wide area outside the City and to maintain the prosperity and life of the City Centre. The Shires improved the attractiveness of the Centre but, by using land that was largely vacant, had a relatively small effect on the existing fabric of the City.

ABOVE Burleys Flyover, 1970

FACING PAGE TOP RIGHT Entrance to the Shires extension from Church Gate 1994

# 39
# *Traffic*

OPINION IS DIVIDED on the question of coping with motor traffic in towns. On the one hand, private motor transport brings people to the City to work and support the local economy. On the other, the increasing volume of traffic has radically changed the shape of the City and poses the most potent threat to the quality of its environment. From the beginnings of the growth of motor traffic cars and lorries were allowed unrestricted access to cities. The partial reversal of this trend has been relatively recent and has taken place against the unpromising background of car ownership forecast to go on rising, established habits and expectations of car use, and decline in public transport.

The restriction of traffic in the central core which has progressed in Leicester in recent years has begun to realise an alternative vision of streets where people on foot take priority. But this vision is practicable only at the cost of massive road construction around the City Centre. Streets like Burleys Way and Vaughan Way afford no pleasure at all to the pedestrian or the cyclist and little to the driver. They have severed an important part of the mediaeval town from the modern City Centre and add nothing to the sense of historical continuity so important for urban living. But it is now difficult to envisage a modern city in which motor traffic was excluded: the effect on the local economy could be disastrous.

The effect which road building has had on the shape of Leicester can be shown by looking at old maps. The 1887 map shows the Burleys Way area as a mass of small plots, houses crammed into courtyards, factories, and pubs. The pattern of ownership would have been as complicated as the street layout. This small scale pattern persisted well into the twentieth

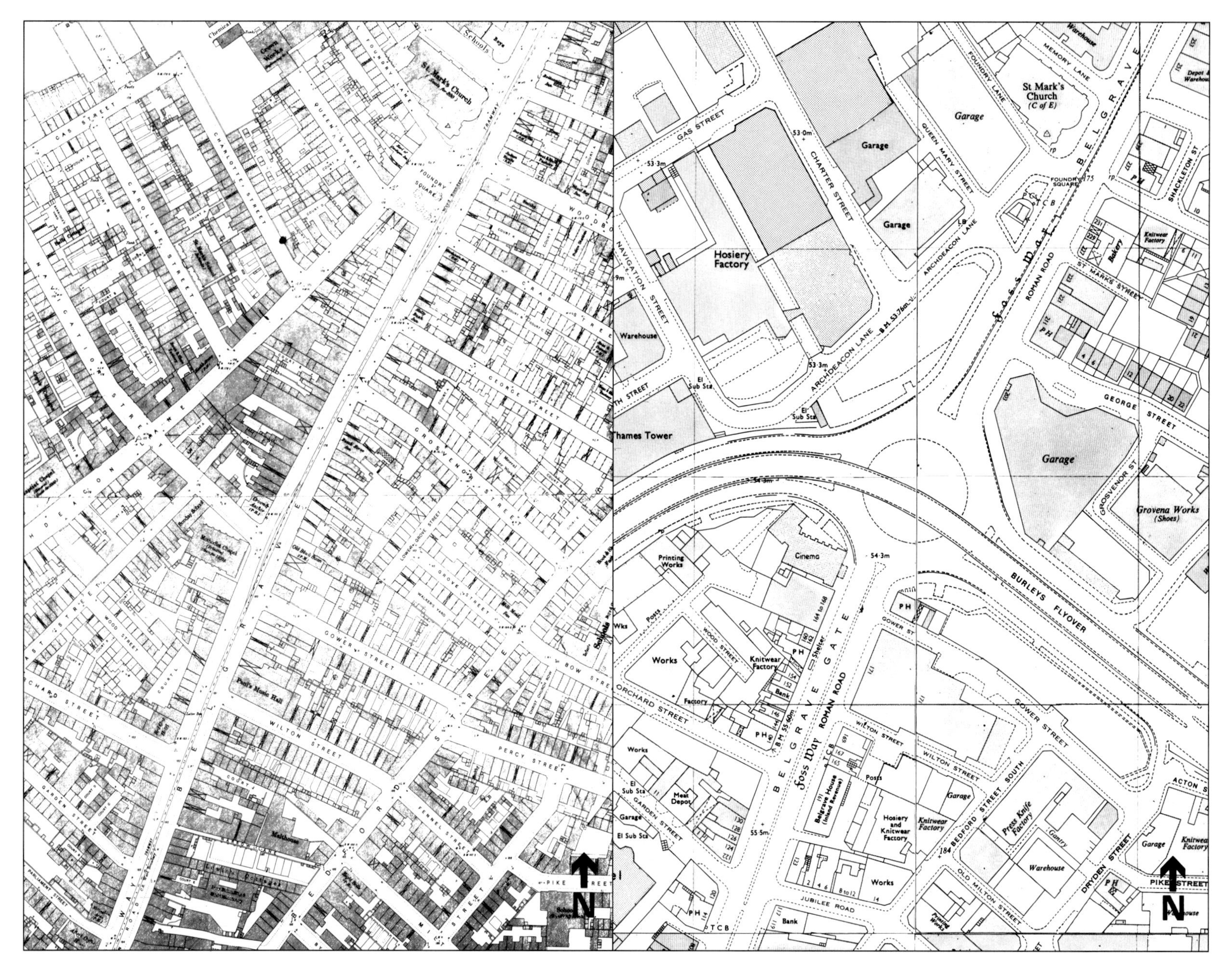


LEFT Extract from the Ordnance Survey map published in 1887 showing Belgrave Gate and St Mark's Church and RIGHT, a 1992 map of the same area printed at the same scale. Note the intricate small-scale pattern of buildings and streets in 1887 and the impact of road building and widening and redevelopment evident on the later map.



0 100

SCALE IN METRES

ABOVE AND RIGHT
Burleys Flyover

LOWER RIGHT Belgrave Flyover, 1974

TOP FAR RIGHT Vaughan Way, 1958, and Burleys Way, 1962: perhaps a necessary convenience for traffic but provided at an incalculable cost to the City's environment and sense of history

century. Today the same area is largely under tarmac and sites adjoining the road have single ownerships and big plots and buildings. It would be quite wrong to romanticise the condition of the area in the late nineteenth century but the maps do illustrate how radically road building has changed the nature of the City.

Not all the effects have been bad: roads have brought some interesting, even exciting, new structures to the City. They may offer the driver a different view of the City but they can also add to the street scene at ground level. Burleys Flyover sweeps across Belgrave Gate with a curve both through the air and across the ground. It was built in 1970 of reinforced concrete cast in place. It is of six spans and, like many road

structures, its most impressive view is from underneath where the sweep of the road deck is supported on massive tapered piers with exposed aggregate surfaces.

Further north past St Mark's Church, Belgrave Flyover, built in 1974, spans half a mile over Belgrave Circle. The precast concrete beams are supported on cross head piers.

Developments in the outer areas of the City and the need to divert through traffic away from the Centre have led to extensive road building in the suburbs. Watermead Way, across the northern fringe of the City between Thurmaston and Birstall, was built in 1974 and included the last bridge to be designed by the old Leicester Corporation before highway responsibilities were taken on for twenty-three years by the County Council. The bridge represented an innovative engineering design.

TOP LEFT Belgrave Flyover with St Mark's Church, 1872

TOP RIGHT Arrows of desire: Central Ring Road, Waterloo Way/ London Road

ABOVE AND LOWER RIGHT Watermead Way Bridge, 1974

BOTTOM Watermead Way Bridge

RIGHT Red Hill Flyover, 1988

The heart of the structure is a hollow box with steel tendons embedded within it. This carries the road deck and is supported on two stout Y-shaped piers which carry the bridge in a gentle arc over the river. Like all the bridges maintained by the City Council the inside of the box is inspected each year by the Council's engineers.

Red Hill Flyover added a new landmark to the northern fringe of the City in 1988. Careful attention has been paid to the texture and appearance of the piers supporting the road but, like many of the best modern engineering structures, its quality lies in the simple, elegant curve of its overall design.

De Montfort University, metal relief panels signed by Percy Brown, entrance doors to Hawthorn Building, 1937

# 40
# *Art and Technology*

THE CITY CAMPUS of De Montfort University has none of the visual coherence or prominence of Leicester University with its group of large buildings on the top of the hill. But this is changing as the younger University gradually gives an overall identity to a disparate collection of buildings and spaces. De Montfort University and its predecessors, the College of Art and Technology and Leicester Polytechnic, have made a profound impression on Leicester in a number of ways. The College and Polytechnic have trained architects, craftspeople and artists, surveyors and conservation specialists, engineers and designers, who have, between them, been instrumental in shaping the City throughout the twentieth century.

The buildings in which these people trained reflect the industrial nature of the City that the original College was founded to serve. The Clephan Building, which houses the School of the Built Environment, was actually built in 1888 as a shoe factory. But it is of a superior Queen Anne design with delightful terracotta sunflowers above the first floor windows.

The first building intended specifically for the College was the Hawthorn Building in the Newarke. It was designed by Everard and Pick in 1896-97 and, like the Clephan Building, it reflects English architecture of about two hundred years earlier. The Hawthorn Building was expanded in several stages up to and into the 1930s, and the style changed to stripped-down Classical as the complex grew. The materials remained similar: orange-red brick with smooth Portland Stone, the latter forming carved relief panels on the 1930s part of the building facing the Newarke.

RIGHT De Montfort University: Clephan, Hawthorn, and James Went Buildings

LOWER RIGHT De Montfort University, terracotta sunflower decoration, Clephan Building, 1888

RIGHT AND FAR RIGHT Portland Stone Relief Panels, Hawthorn Building

BELOW RIGHT Portland Building, 1888

The buildings of the 1960s seemed to try as hard as they could to be indistinguishable from the offices which were booming at the time. Neither the Fletcher Building of 1966 nor the James Went Building of 1966-73, both built by the Corporation, provided a distinctive focus around which the Polytechnic, and now the University, could group. Even so, the Fletcher Building goes some way towards providing a formal square and the James Went Building provides interest from the Newarke by the pattern and activity of its stair towers.

Several of the civic buildings of the 1970s were in hard, smooth red brick. The Kimberlin Library was one of these and, if the brick adds to the somewhat forbidding external experience, the tall

ABOVE James Went Building, 1966-73, and Gateway School

TOP FAR RIGHT James Went Building

RIGHT Sunblinds and cedar shingles added to Fletcher Building in 1992

LOWER RIGHT Extension to Kimberlin Library 1997

narrow windows do at least reflect the function of the building in which the emphasis is on quiet concentration on the material inside.

In recent years the Polytechnic/University has tried to improve the image of the campus. This is no easy task but a start has been made and the University has commissioned striking work by nationally-known architects. Alterations to existing buildings have been another way in which the University has tried to establish a common design theme. One of the most dramatic examples is provided by the sun blinds that add a pattern of chevrons and a ship-like quality to Gateway House.

The Queens Building, housing the School of Engineering and Manufacture, gives the University a real landmark. Designed by Peake Short and Partners (now Short Ford and Associates) of London, it is one of the most extraordinary buildings ever to appear in Leicester, or, indeed, in twentieth century Britain. Faced in red and buff brick and cedar shingles, its apparently rambling design is disciplined by the need to conserve energy, warming the building by the heat generated by the machines and people inside, and cooling it by exploiting the natural air flow. It is one of the largest naturally-ventilated buildings in Europe. By contrast, many conventional office buildings of the 1960s and 1970s, built at a time when energy was cheap, rely entirely on electricity for heating and ventilation.

TOP Student Health Centre 1992

ABOVE Hawthorn Building 1896-97 and The Newarke

RIGHT Sunblinds fixed to Gateway House as part of conversion scheme carried out from 1989

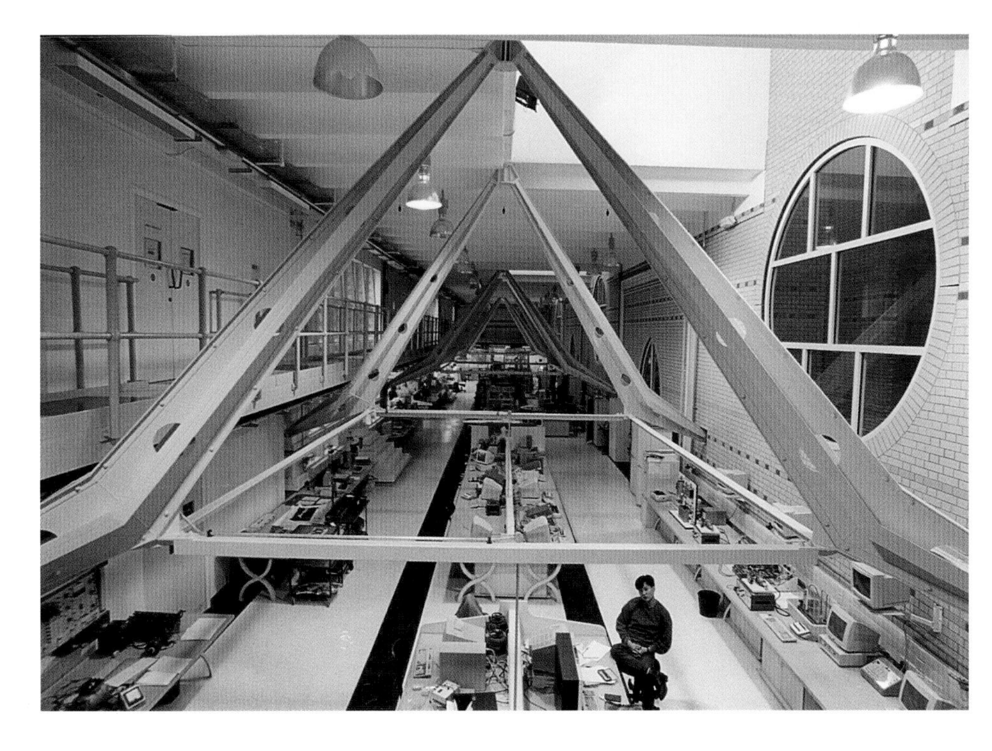

Like Leicester University Engineering Building of thirty years earlier the Queens Building reflects themes from the City around it. This is evident both in the use of materials on the outside, and in the formation of a superb, lofty internal space to echo the former street pattern of the Mill Lane area.

ABOVE, TOP AND FAR RIGHT
Queens Building, Mill Lane

RIGHT AND BELOW
Queens Building south side

FACING PAGE Queens Building, internal concourse

Since the opening of the Queens Building in 1993 De Montfort University has continued to pursue a progressive policy in the design of its new buildings. The Health Centre of 1992 is by Bundey and Rodgers of Market Harborough (a practice whose expertise with health buildings has been recognised by an award from the Royal Institute of British Architects). It is built in white concrete blocks bringing an almost North African feel to a formerly inhospitable space.

The pressure on library facilities caused by the growth of student numbers has led to the extension to the Kimberlin Library by Eva Jiricna, a prominent London architects' practice. The design approach is cool and sophisticated with regular clean-cut window openings and grey tiles forming the external finish.

The De Montfort University campus has some way to go before it can really be seen as architecturally unified, but it already illustrates some important points. Although the Queens Building received a mixed critical response in the architectural world, the building teaches one important lesson especially well. Like Stirling and Gowan at Leicester University before them, Short Ford show that echoing local themes in new building need not produce dull results. The very diversity of the character of British towns and cities can provide the starting point for varied and highly original buildings which can excite the eye and the imagination.

# 41
# *The Future*

SOME READERS may have come to the last chapter of *The Quality of Leicester* without finding their favourite building or street. We have tried to give an idea of the range of street scenes, open spaces, buildings, and details of buildings, which together present something of the character of the City. What has been left out could show the extent of Leicester's variety and quality as much as the examples which have been included.

One thing should be clear: the idea of the *character* of Leicester, or of any other place, is hard to define. Buildings, streets, and spaces are part of it, so are the uses to which buildings are put. Rocks and soil and local climate have determined the range of building materials and the way in which they were used. But the history of Leicester and its citizens is the force which has moulded the shape of the City and given it life.

It is especially hard to pin down this notion of *character* because it is always changing and must continue to change. Even the oldest parts of Leicester are a patchwork of building work from many periods. This book is a portrait of Leicester at the turning point of a century and millennium. What we may see at one time as a still snapshot is really much more like a frame in a moving film. Changes in people's lives, and the technology which makes change possible, call for constant adaptation in the environment, and the City must adapt to live. The Council, and everyone involved in the development of the City, is charged with managing change in a way which respects Leicester's historic fabric. There need be no conflict between conservation and new development; they are complementary activities which share the same goal. *The Quality of Leicester* has shown that the rich and intricate pattern of a historic city can be the basis for building an urban environment of high quality.

A book focusing on the built environment inevitably tends to emphasise architects. The architect's name is often the main thing known about an older building but architects are not the only people who shape the character of a city. It is formed also by the clients and institutions who finance development, by the people who use and change buildings, by engineers, builders and craftspeople, planners, business people, politicians, and anyone who lives or works in the city.

We have mentioned the steps which the City Council has taken, and encouraged others to take, to shape an environment within which people with disabilities can move as freely as possible. The lead that Leicester took in this in the early 1980s has been followed by many other towns and cities throughout the country.

Women have contributed to the City's character as patrons and users of buildings, as architects, artists, and planners. But, at least until recent years, the environment has been formed mainly by men and has largely reflected men's needs. Fairness and equality alone demand a change in this imbalance.

There is another powerful reason why all groups in the City's community must play their part in protecting and building on the quality of Leicester. The developing character of the City will be a product of the life of its people. Influences from a wide variety of cultures on the character of Leicester have been a constant theme in the book and are a vital dynamic force in the further development of the City. Creativity is especially fertile when cultures and ideas meet and draw from each other. Leicester, with its wide variety of ethnic groups, religions, art, music, and community and economic life is ideally placed to build a rich and rewarding future. As the City moves into its third millennium the character formed by the work of previous centuries will be enhanced. More than ever, Leicester will become a special place.

RIGHT Jewry Wall, summer 1992

FACING PAGE Western Park, November 1992

# *Afterword to 1993 Edition by John Dean*
## *City Planning Officer 1973 - 1993*

In this book we have tried to reveal something of the special qualities of Leicester. Concerns for the past and the buildings we have inherited have come to be matters of growing importance over the past twenty years or so. We cannot see these values diminishing, rather they will become stronger. But they are values which do not yet sufficiently influence the way we invest in buildings. Too often something of the quality of Leicester must be lost; 'the market' does not respond as it should.

Also through this book we want to influence new design, in which context should be a primary consideration. To reveal local quality will provide us with a sense of place.

Jewry Wall and St Nicholas' Church: some light on the past

SPACE - STREET - BUILDING - DETAIL

RIGHT Abbey Park

FAR RIGHT Guildhall Lane

BELOW

RIGHT Leicester University: The Richard Attenborough Centre for Disability and the Arts

FAR RIGHT The Town Hall

# Bibliography

We are pleased to acknowledge the following sources of information, which have been used in the preparation of *The Quality of Leicester*, and to recommend them as further reading.


Helen Boynton and Grant Pitches *Desirable Locations: Leicester's Middle Class Suburbs 1880-1920* Leicester City Council (Living History Unit) 1996

Geoff Brandwood and Martin Cherry *Men of Property: the Goddards and Six Generations of Architecture* Leicestershire Museums, Arts and Records Service 1990

A. E. Brown (Ed.) *The Growth of Leicester* Leicester University Press 1970

Annette Carruthers *Ernest Gimson and the Cotswold Group of Craftsmen* Leicestershire Museums 1978

Paul and Yolanda Courtney *The Changing Face of Leicester* Alan Sutton Stroud 1995

Patrick Clay *Leicester before the Romans* Leicestershire Museums, Art Galleries and Records Service 1988

James Stevens Curl 'City of Giant Orders: Neo-Classical Leicester' *Country Life* Vol.CLXXXIV No.4489 1st September 1983 pp 564-567

Malcolm Elliott *Victorian Leicester* Phillimore London and Chichester 1979

Colin Ellis *History in Leicester* City of Leicester Publicity Department 1948 (and later editions)

E. J. Emery *The History of Abbey Park, Leicester* Leicester City Council 1982

Jean Farquhar *Arthur Wakerley 1862-1931* Sedgebrook 1984

Richard Gill *The Book of Leicester* Barracuda Buckingham 1985

Mark Girouard *The English Town* Yale University Press New Haven and London 1990

Mark Girouard *Sweetness and Light: the Queen Anne Movement 1860-1900* Oxford University Press 1977

W. G. Hoskins *The Making of the English Landscape* Penguin Harmondsworth 1970 (and other editions)

W.G. Hoskins *A Shell Guide: Leicestershire* Faber and Faber London 1970

Pat Kirkham *Harry Peach: Dryad and the DIA.* The Design Council London 1986

Leicester City Council *Leicester's Architectural Heritage* Leicester City Council 1975

Leicester City Council *Leicester Ecology Strategy Part One* Leicester City Council 1989

Leicester City Council *Renewal Strategies: First Report* Leicester City Council 1975

Leicester City Council *Riverside Park* Leicester City Council 1986

Leicester City Council *William Lee's Legacy: the Leicester Knitting Trail* Leicester City Council 1989

Leicestershire County Council *The Local Tradition* Leicestershire County Council 1975

R. J. B. Keene *Architecture in Leicestershire 1834-1984* Leicestershire and Rutland Society of Architects 1984

John McKean *Leicester University Engineering Building* Phaidon London 1994

David Nash and David Reeder (Eds.) *Leicester in the Twentieth Century* Alan Sutton/Leicester City Council Stroud 1993

John Nichols *The History and Antiquities of the County of Leicester* 4 Vols. 1795-1805. Re-published by S. R. Publishers and Leicestershire County Council 1971

Nikolaus Pevsner and Elizabeth Williamson *The Buildings of England: Leicestershire and Rutland* 2nd Edition Penguin Harmondsworth 1984

Jack Simmons *Leicester Past and Present Vol.1: The Ancient Borough to 1860 Vol.2: Modern City 1860-1974* Eyre Methuen London 1974

Susanna Watts *A Walk through Leicester* 1804 Facsimile edition published by Leicester University Press 1967

J. H. McD. Whitaker *The Building Stones of Leicester: a City Trail* Leicestershire Museums, Art Galleries and Records Service 1981

Bill Willbond *A Home of Our Own: Seventy Years of Council House Memories in Leicester* Leicester City Council 1991

Daniel Williams (Ed.) *The Adaptation of Change: Essays upon the Nineteenth Century History of Leicester and Leicestershire* Leicestershire Museums, Art Galleries and Records Service 1980

Jonathan Wilshire *Old Braunstone* Chamberlain Leicester 1983

Jonathan Wilshire *Old Evington* Chamberlain Leicester 1983

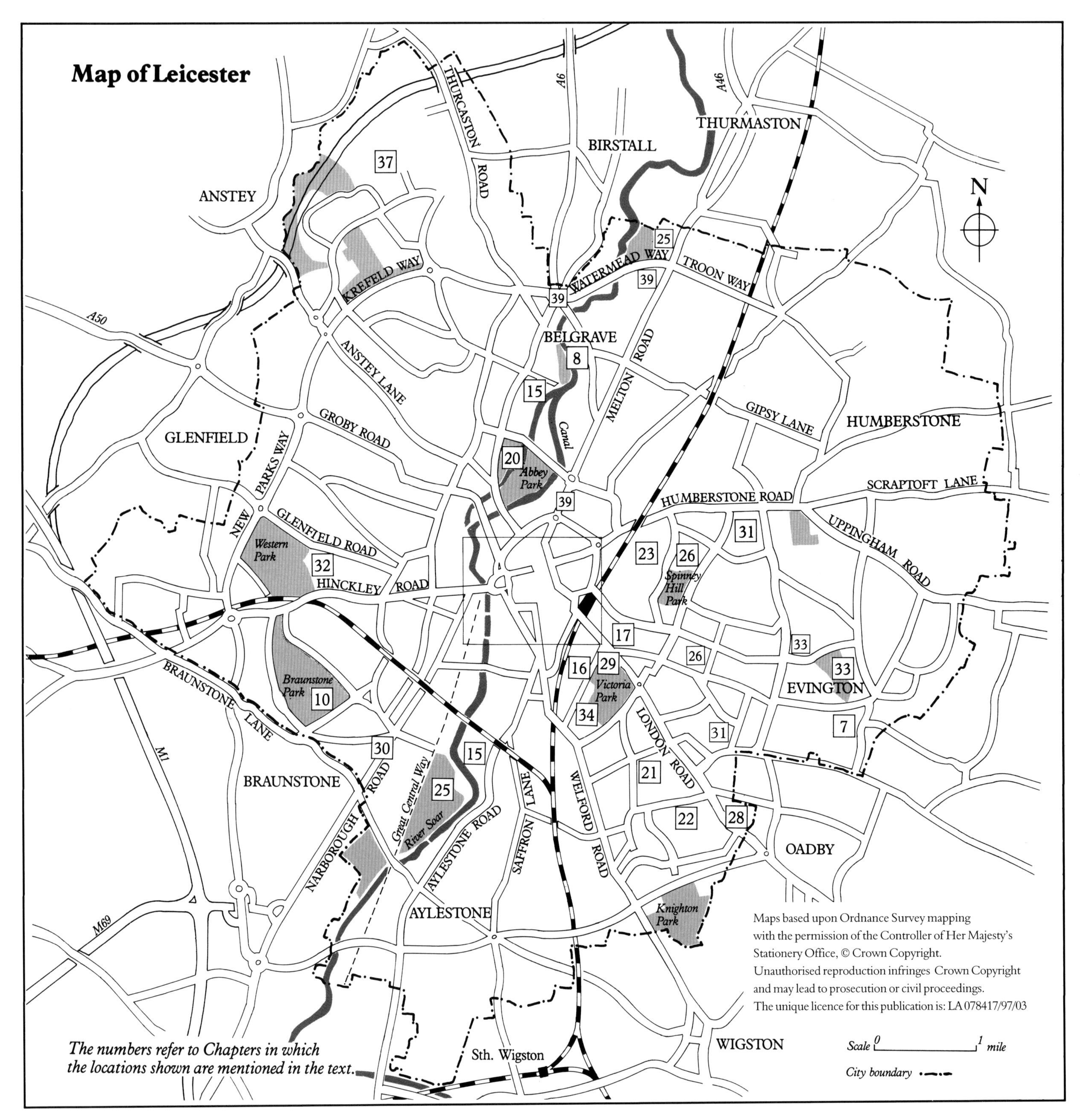
Map of Leicester
N
THURCASTON ROAD
A6
A46
THURMASTON
BIRSTALL
37
ANSTEY
25
WATERMEAD WAY
TROON WAY
KREFELD WAY
39
A50
BELGRAVE
8
ANSTEY LANE
MELTON ROAD
15
GIPSY LANE
HUMBERSTONE
GLENFIELD
NEW PARKS WAY
GROBY ROAD
Canal
20
Abbey Park
SCRAPTOFT LANE
HUMBERSTONE ROAD
GLENFIELD ROAD
Western Park
32
HINCKLEY ROAD
31
23
26
Spinney Hill Park
UPPINGHAM ROAD
17
33
26
16
29
Victoria Park
33
EVINGTON
BRAUNSTONE LANE
Braunstone Park
10
34
LONDON ROAD
31
7
30
M1
BRAUNSTONE
NARBOROUGH ROAD
Great Central Way
River Soar
25
15
AYLESTONE ROAD
SAFFRON LANE
WELFORD ROAD
21
22
28
OADBY
AYLESTONE
Knighton Park
M69
Sth. Wigston
WIGSTON
Scale 0 1 mile
City boundary
The numbers refer to Chapters in which the locations shown are mentioned in the text.
Maps based upon Ordnance Survey mapping with the permission of the Controller of Her Majesty's Stationery Office, © Crown Copyright.
Unauthorised reproduction infringes Crown Copyright and may lead to prosecution or civil proceedings.
The unique licence for this publication is: LA 078417/97/03

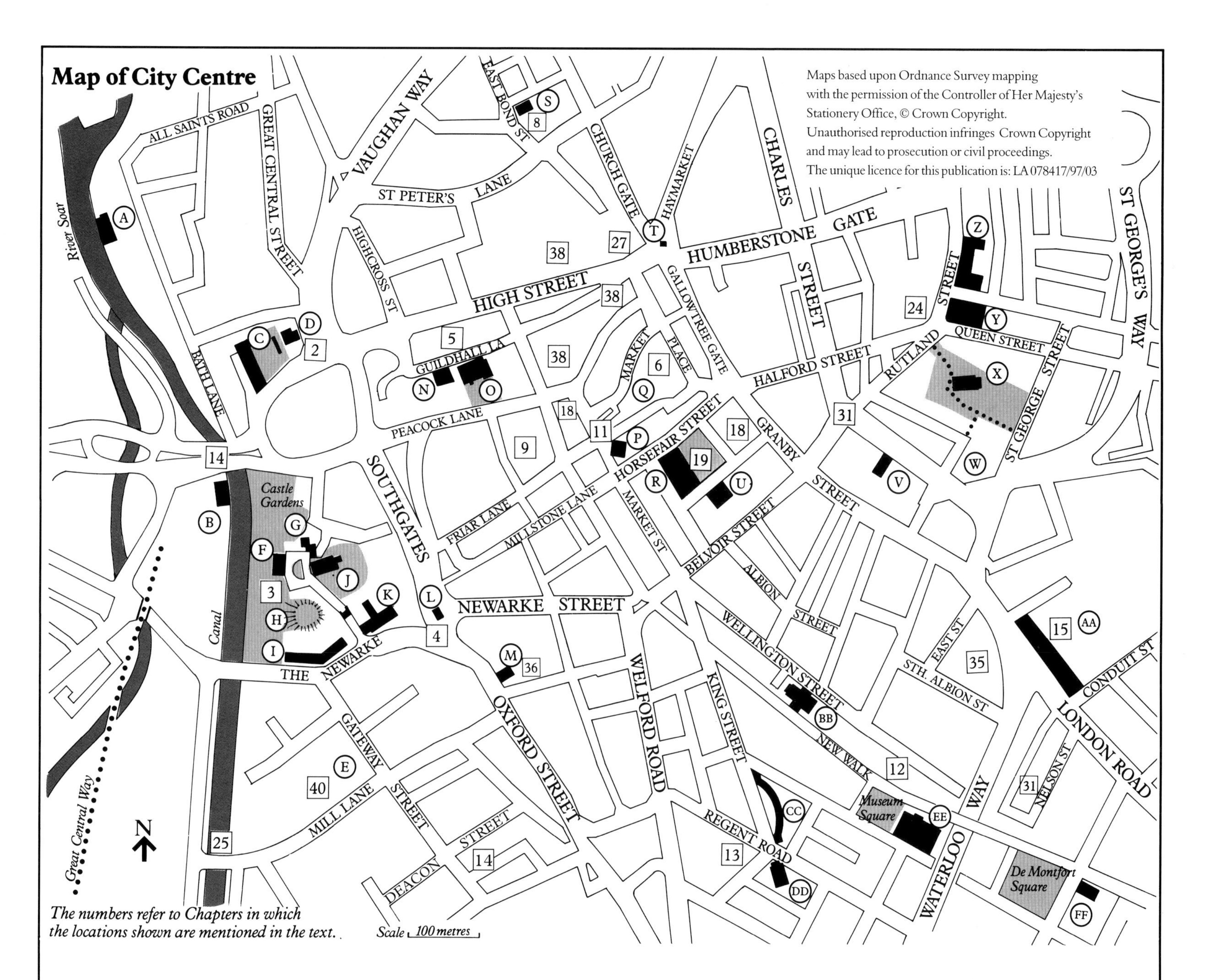


| | | | | | | | |
|---|---|---|---|---|---|---|---|
| A | Friars Mills | I | Trinity Hospital | Q | Market | Y | Odeon Cinema |
| B | Pex (West Bridge Place) | J | St Mary de Castro Church | R | Town Hall | Z | Alexandra House |
| C | Jewry Wall | K | Newarke Houses | S | Great Meeting Church | AA | Railway Station |
| D | St Nicholas' Church | L | Magazine Gateway | T | Clock Tower | BB | Holy Cross Priory |
| E | De Montfort University | M | Jain Centre | U | Bishop St. Methodist Church | CC | The Crescent |
| F | The Castle | N | Guildhall | V | United Baptist Church | DD | Holy Trinity Church |
| G | Castle Gatehouse | O | Cathedral | W | Police Station | EE | Museum |
| H | Castle Mound | P | City Rooms | X | St George's Church | FF | St Stephen's Church |

# Index

## C

## D



## E



## F



## G

## H



## I



## J

## S



## T

## U



## V



## W



## Y

# NOTES

# NOTES

# NOTES